Medieval Literature: A Very Short Introduction

VERY SHORT INTRODUCTIONS are for anyone wanting a stimulating and accessible way into a new subject. They are written by experts, and have been translated into more than 40 different languages.

The series began in 1995, and now covers a wide variety of topics in every discipline. The VSI library now contains over 400 volumes—a Very Short Introduction to everything from Psychology and Philosophy of Science to American History and Relativity—and continues to grow in every subject area.

## Very Short Introductions available now:

**Available soon:**

### For more information visit our website

www.oup.com/vsi/

Elaine Treharne

# MEDIEVAL LITERATURE

A Very Short Introduction

OXFORD
UNIVERSITY PRESS

# OXFORD
UNIVERSITY PRESS

Great Clarendon Street, Oxford, OX2 6DP,
United Kingdom

Oxford University Press is a department of the University of Oxford.
It furthers the University's objective of excellence in research, scholarship,
and education by publishing worldwide. Oxford is a registered trade mark of
Oxford University Press in the UK and in certain other countries

© Elaine Treharne 2015

The moral rights of the author have been asserted

First edition published in 2015

Impression: 1

Published in the United States of America by Oxford University Press
198 Madison Avenue, New York, NY 10016, United States of America

British Library Cataloguing in Publication Data
Data available

Library of Congress Control Number: 2015935245

ISBN 978-0-19-966849-6

Printed in Great Britain by
Ashford Colour Press Ltd, Gosport, Hampshire

*For my Mum, Iola Treharne*
*and*
*in memory of my Dad, Kenneth Treharne*

# Contents

# Acknowledgements

This short work builds on a great deal of wonderful medieval scholarship read and absorbed over thirty years. Because there are no footnotes in these little books, my debt is indicated only in part by the Further reading provided at the end. I thank my fellow medievalists for their dynamism, passion, and inspirational scholarship. Medieval Studies is the best of fields. In particular, I thank Benjamin Albritton, Orietta Da Rold, Jill Frederick, Andrew Prescott, Kathryn Starkey, and Greg Walker for their friendship and support. Special thanks to Dr George Younge, who kindly and perceptively read a draft of this book. I am grateful for the helpful critiques of the OUP readers and my editor, Jenny Nugee. To my family—Andrew, Jonathan, and Isabel Fryett—you are the epitome of patience, joy, and love: thank you.

# List of illustrations

# Introduction: endings and beginnings

Medieval literature in Britain and Ireland spans over a thousand years from the Fall of Rome in *c.*410 CE to the shifting tides of the Renaissance in the 15th and 16th centuries. This millennium-long period is marked by conversion, conquest, crusade, and cultural innovation, all of which dramatically influenced the literature that emerged, leaving us with a rich and fascinating textual legacy.

At the beginning of the 5th century, Rome fell to the attacking Visigoths sweeping down into Italy from the north. This heralded the gradual demise of one of the greatest empires in world history. The Roman Empire, which at its apogee extended from Northern England to Egypt and the Caspian Sea to the Iberian Peninsula, had become Christian in the 4th century under the emperor Constantine; where countries were subject to imperial rule, Christianity was declared the official religion. Within a century, though, Christianity was under pressure from polytheism, like the northern tribes' veneration of Germanic and Norse gods, and within the next few centuries, Islam began its push across the southern and western Mediterranean.

Britain during these centuries was always at least partly Christian: after the Roman garrisons were called back to Rome in the early 5th century, those parts of Britain that had been under Roman rule remained essentially Christian, until the pagan Angles,

Saxons, Jutes, and Frisians, who came from modern day northern Germany, Denmark, and the Low Countries, displaced the indigenous Christian Celts. In the preceding 500 years, though, during its heyday, Rome and its citizens had produced a vast body of literature—both Christian and secular—whose influence has never really waned subsequently; moreover, the Empire had provided a social, military, and administrative coherence to much of Europe and the Mediterranean that is still evident in its material remains from Hadrian's Wall to the ancient cities of Antioch and Marseilles. The decline of Rome effectively led to the fragmentation of Europe, during which time peoples migrated, new nation states were formed, and vernacular languages, like English, German, French, and Spanish eventually took on separate identities that were recorded in writing for the first time from the 7th to the 12th centuries.

The British Isles—that is, the modern Republic of Ireland, Wales, England, Scotland, Northern Ireland, and the smaller islands all around the coast—have complex political and historical stories to tell. For Britain specifically, the centuries immediately following the decline of the Roman Empire gave rise to the countries now defined as Wales, Scotland, and England. During the 5th century, the Angles, Saxons, Jutes, and Frisians, who had initially been invited to assist local kings in the Celts' internecine wars, decided to stay and were joined by others. There was no peaceful rapprochement between these settlers and the Celts, who were pushed back from all parts of Britain to the western fringes of the island. They went on to form the dominant population of Wales (the term itself derived from 'wealas', Old English 'wealh' denoting a 'foreigner, a Celt'), Cornwall, and Brittany.

The Anglo-Saxon invader-settlers formed a variety of kingdoms, and it was not until about the 10th century that England, as we now know it, was established (see Figure 1). Even then, from the late 8th century, there was also the tricky issue of the Vikings to

**1. Map of early Britain.**

deal with. These Norsemen first invaded in 793, but ultimately settled in the east and north of England, west Wales, eastern Ireland, and parts of Scotland. Indeed, Scotland itself also emerged from competing rivalries—here, chiefly among the Picts, the Scotti, and the English—and faced numerous other tumultuous events into the later Middle Ages.

These territorial and political struggles for control in England, Scotland, Wales, and Ireland continued throughout the medieval period, too, though by the 11th century, the boundaries of the countries involved were well established. The Scandinavian Conquest under Cnut in 1016, and the Norman Conquest by William in October 1066, brought notable change to England's government immediately, though the Norman settlement had, over time, a major impact on all areas of Britain and Ireland, and all facets of culture and society.

In these centuries, Britain and Ireland witnessed important innovation, from the establishment of the universities of Oxford, Cambridge, and St Andrews, to the emergence of new religious orders, like the Cistercians and the Dominican and Franciscan Friars. Literacy and bureaucracy increased with each passing century, and urbanization brought about the development of a professional middle class. Trade and travel became more common as the decades progressed, and scholarly and international exchange was part of this process. Towards the end of the medieval period (which came earlier in continental Europe than in the British Isles), composing literature could be a profession for some, with notable authors like the Italians Petrarch, Dante, and Boccaccio making a particularly notable contribution to developing secularized literature. The gradual emergence of Parliament in England, and wholesale shifts in the economy, directly affected by catastrophic events like the Black Death in the 14th century, meant that society in the later Middle Ages had been dramatically altered from that of some 400 years earlier.

## The Dark Ages

Medieval Literature is not solely born of a warrior-obsessed Dark Ages. Indeed, a 'dark' age suggests dimness, a hiatus in high culture, and a lack of accomplishment. Coined first by Italian Renaissance scholars, like Petrarch, to indicate the enlightenment brought about by the re-emergence of classical learning in their 14th- and 15th-century world, the metaphor of the 'Dark Ages' went on to be used, unhelpfully, to describe some or all of the period between the 5th and 15th centuries, when, it was thought, classical learning was subordinated—suppressed even. This is not an accurate view of the period; neither is the modern disparaging use of the word 'medieval' helpful. These unfavourable labels cannot be applied realistically to an entire millennium, nor do they represent the period and its peoples.

Considering the medieval period as a whole means being able to scan the immense variety and complexity of literary production in its fullness, a fullness that includes multiple languages (including Cornish, English, French, Irish, Latin, Old Norse, Welsh), many thousands of manuscripts and inscribed textual objects, and very different cultures of literacy. Manuscripts exist from the British Isles as early as the 7th century, but even these texts were pre-empted by runic, Ogham, and Pictish inscriptions on various artefacts. The runic alphabet, the Germanic *fuþorc* (named after the initial six characters), belonged to the Anglo-Saxons and other Germanic tribes before the Anglo-Saxons settled on the island of Britain. This alphabet consisted of about thirty graphs shaped ideally for carving. Each of these both had its own meaning and represented a sound. Thus, *þ*, a character that was adopted into the Old English writing system, represented <th> and is called 'thorn', which means precisely that—'thorn'. Another graph, *p*, called *wynn*, was used in Old English writings to represent the modern graph <w>, and *wynn* itself means 'joy'.

Runic writing was associated not only with literacy, but also a meditative sensibility, a wisdom that reflected the specialized access of only a very few people to reading and writing. To be able to read, and then to write, implied a high level of education that necessarily set those skilled in these arts apart from the vast majority of others. This is true in all literature cultures, including early Celtic societies in Wales, Ireland, the southwest of England, Scotland and the Isle of Man. There, Ogham script dating from about the 4th century onwards was used to record Irish and British texts in sequences of linear strokes or dots carved individually across and down a central vertical line. Some Ogham stones are, rather helpfully, bilingual and include Latin alongside the Ogham script, which helps as an interpretation aid. Most of these objects inscribe names of people together with some brief details about the land of these people or their lineage. People's desire to leave some record of having existed here in this world is often the impetus for the earliest writings, as true in terms of inscription on stone and bone markers and objects as it is for fully-fledged 'literature' a few hundred years later.

## Early literary issues

'Literature', derived from Latin 'litteratura' meaning 'use, or systems, of writing', is represented in its earliest British and Irish forms in these signs of the Ogham and Runic inscriptions. The function and meaning of many such inscriptions are mysterious, but no less 'literary' for that. One is a very famous 8th-century rectangular whalebone casket called the Franks Casket, discovered in the 19th century and now in the British Museum, though one panel is in Florence. On this box, illustrative scenes carved in relief are framed by lines of runes and roman letters.

Made in Northumbria, the Franks Casket raises issues that can illuminate the literary Middle Ages as a whole. The casket's juxtaposition of the legendary Germanic smith, Weland, on the left-hand side of the front panel with the birth of Christ on the right might have reminded viewers of the conversion of some of the Germanic peoples from paganism to Christianity. This took place in parts of Northern Europe, beginning for the Anglo-Saxons at the end of the 6th century (remembering, though, that the British and Irish Celts had been Christian since the 4th century). From the perspective of the Franks Casket as a whole object, the runic and roman letters carved around the panels in a mixture of Old English and Latin show the richness, multilingualism, and complexity of this early literary culture.

On another scale, the Ruthwell Cross, made around 700 CE, is a monumental preaching cross, now preserved inside Ruthwell Church, near Dumfries in Scotland (see Figure 2). This area was originally part of Anglo-Saxon England in the early medieval period, and this cross has carved panels that show a combination of Christian and Germanic cultures, including Christ trampling the beasts, Mary Magdalene attending to Christ, Saints Anthony and Paul, and vine-scrolls. Runic and roman alphabet inscriptions frame some of these scenes, and a remarkable runic inscription is written around some panels, with words that herald the longer, 10th-century Old English poem about Jesus' crucifixion and resurrection—*The Dream of the Rood*. These runes tell of a courageous Christ, ready to ascend the Cross to redeem mankind: 'geredæ hinæ God almehttig | þa he walde of galgu gistiga | modig fore allæ men' ('God almighty stripped himself, | when he wanted to climb the Cross, | brave before all men'). On the Ruthwell Cross, we see the combination of image and word, Germanic rune and Christian subject, anonymous authors and artists, public communal text and demand for personal contemplation. These components illustrate aspects of literary production that remain throughout the medieval period, though in different combinations at different times.

This was a period of gradual change, then; of long-lived traditions like those around the pagan Germanic polytheistic religion coming into direct contact with the powerful Christian mission. Very few people were literate, but the letters familiar to those who were educated had prestige and power. Literary and

2. The Ruthwell Cross.

artistic production in the Middle Ages was often the responsibility of monasteries and those associated with the church, but it is seldom known when or where a good number of the surviving texts and objects were made, or, indeed, by whom or for whom they were created. Authors are more often than not anonymous, the audiences unknowable, and inherited learning—'auctoritee' ('authority')—immensely significant. As a result, the literary remains we do have are almost always a challenge and can be quite difficult to interpret. Like the damaged Ruthwell Cross, many of the medieval texts that have been left to modern readers are incomplete or fragmentary; some exist only in copies made much later; some are known to have existed, but are now lost. But, that said, *all* is not lost; plenty of textual relics survive.

## The big questions

From the beginnings of the medieval period, the same big questions that all of humanity asks play a major role in the composition of poetry, prose, and drama. Despite the foreignness of early languages, and the occasional distance created by social and political *mores* no longer seen in our contemporary world, the familiarity of the subject matter of medieval literature underpins much of the literary composition: the need to declare victory and praise those in power, to mourn loss, to enact laws; the desire to utter truths and acquire wisdom; the urge to express love or hatred.

Writers, from the unknown poet(s) of the Ruthwell Cross to the most famous of authors, Geoffrey Chaucer, in his magisterial 14th-century romance *Troilus and Criseyde*, showed through their literary creations that the things of this world are transient, mutable, uncertain, and that humans pass through this world in the blink of an eye. What, then, is life for? What purpose do humans serve? How can those in power seek to control those around them? How do we attain peace, salvation? How can we strive to live a meaningful life? Literature of the Middle Ages

## Box 1 Welsh literature

While very few early texts survive before c.1100, the evidence that does exist from later manuscripts suggests that the earliest works in Welsh, attributable to Taliesin and Aneirin, might be dated to the 6th century. Welsh authors wrote in Latin throughout the period: Gildas is the first known writer; and Nennius' 9th-century *Historia Brittonum* (containing the primary reference to King Arthur), for example, provides initial evidence for a literary tradition in Wales. Welsh poems of the later 9th or early 10th centuries are recorded in the margins of a Latin verse version of the Gospels; and the remains of *englynion* (Welsh verse) also survive in the upper margin of a stunning manuscript of Augustine's *De Trinitate* made in the 11th century.

After the 12th century, Welsh texts survive in many manuscripts. Welsh poetry flourished in the High Middle Ages, patronized, and also written, by princes and the gentry. Among the most famous poets are Dafydd ap Gwilym and Iolo Goch. Welsh prose in many genres exists, too, including prophecies, histories, lawcodes, and romances. Perhaps the most famous medieval work is the set of texts known as the *Mabinogion*, which relates the mythological history of the Celts.

addresses these questions through a variety of genres in a multitude of languages and forms.

For Siôn Cent, a 15th-century Welsh poet (see Box 1), life is concerned with appreciating how transitory all earthly things are and yet how glorious the heroes or infamous the sinners of the past. 'Mae'r byd oll? Mawr bu dwyllwr' he states ('Where's all the world? It's been a deceiver') in his poem, *Hud a Lliw y Byd* (*The Illusion of this World*). He asks of all the great subjects of literature: Where's Adam? Where's Arthur, Alexander, Guinevere, Vivien, Herod, Charlemagne, King Richard, Owain, Brutus?

Felly'r byd hwn, gwn ganwaith,
*That's this world, I know it well,*
hud a lliw, nid gwiw ein gwaith.
*magic and colour; our work's of no avail.*

For Siôn Cent, the only certainty and value to life is the maintenance of a keen eye on the afterlife, on learning to concentrate not on worldly goods and the acquisition of knowledge or splendour, but on being faithful and loyal to God. While this pervasive religious core that inspires so much of the literature produced in the Middle Ages can be tricky for modern readers, it should be considered one of the ways in which medieval people tried to understand and fathom their place in the world. The same desire to know the meaning of life and how we fit in with this world around us is yet an unbroken thread connecting all humanity. It is a desire expressed in riddles and elegies, sermons and morality plays, romances and histories, and it is to an explication of these that we now turn.

# Chapter 1
# Literary origins

The history of medieval literature in the British Isles begins at an end, the end of the society belonging to the Britons, as far as the historian Gildas was concerned in his *De excidio et conquestu Britanniae* (*On the Ruin and Conquest of Britain*). This early medieval author, writing in Latin around 550 CE, tells the story of the coming of the Anglo-Saxons in 450 CE and the consequent demise of the British nation, framing these momentous historical events within the context of a divine plan. The Britons, who had been Christianized under Roman imperial rule in the earlier 4th century, had not, according to Gildas, lived the godly lives they should.

Gildas thus shows in his part-history, part-sermon, how God sought to punish the sinful British through their subordination to the Anglo-Saxon invaders. For Gildas, writing in Latin (see Box 2), trained in the early Celtic Christian church, the Britons' momentous defeat at the swords of the Anglo-Saxons came about through 'God being willing to purify his family'. Gildas reveals that in seeking protection for the country after the Roman army left, the British king, Vortigern, and his counsellors, effectively 'sealed its doom by inviting in among them like wolves into the sheep-fold, the fierce and impious Saxons, a race hateful both to God and men, to repel the invasions of the northern nations. Nothing was ever so pernicious to our country, nothing was ever so unlucky.'

## Box 2 Anglo-Latin literature

Throughout the medieval period, Latin was the language of the church, the language of learning, and the language that bound all of western Europe together. Almost all those who lived in Britain and Ireland after Christianization would have heard and participated to some degree in Latinate culture—even if it was only to say an approximate version of the *Pater noster*, the Lord's Prayer. Complex relationships between Latin and the other literary languages of the British Isles are seen in the production of many manuscripts with Latin main texts, and glosses in English or Welsh or Irish; in the translation and adaptation of major Latin works in various vernaculars; and in the macaronic verse of the later Middle Ages, which provides a perfect metrical and stylistic balance between languages.

Every conceivable genre of literature survives in Latin, including the most obvious kinds of liturgical and didactic texts to histories, regulatory works, administrative documents, and lawcodes. Some of the greatest theological and philosophical writers were products of and contributors to the medieval worldview, such as Bede, Anselm, and Robert Grossteste; and a good deal of the most informative and entertaining medieval writing is found in the historical and observational works of authors such as William of Malmesbury, Gerald of Wales, and Ranulf Higden.

Reading the demise of the Romano-Celtic world as God's retribution for the Britons' own inattention to living a Christian life was Gildas's way of understanding the terrible events of the later 5th and earlier 6th centuries. This period of displacement and resettlement will have been a gradual process, but the relative paucity of Celtic words in Old, Middle, and Modern English suggests minimal contact between Anglo-Saxons and Celts on any equal cultural footing. A few Celtic words in English survive: 'brock' ('badger'), 'binn' ('basket'), 'dry' ('magician'). In addition, the frequent relabelling of place-names and topography by Anglo-Saxons suggests that the subordination of the Celts was fairly comprehensive. Surviving place-names of Celtic origin include 'Cornwall', 'Carlisle', 'cumb(e)' for a 'valley', and 'London'.

The low number of words and place-names from Celtic is in sharp contrast to the many hundreds of words that were introduced into English from Latin, particularly once the Anglo-Saxons had been Christianized. The unequal relationship between the Celtic population and the Anglo-Saxon colonists might also be suggested through literary sources. A troubling riddle from the important 10th-century Old English manuscript, the Exeter Book (Exeter Cathedral Library, 3501), reveals, rather bawdily, one particular role of a *wealh* ('foreigner', 'Welsh person') in later Anglo-Saxon England. The object of the riddle (known as Riddle 12) speaks for itself in the first person, giving clues to its identity:

> Fotum Ic fere,    foldan slite,
> *I travel by foot, slice the ground,*
> grene wongas,    þenden Ic gæst bere.
> *the green fields, as long as I bear a spirit.*
> Gif me feorh losað,    fæste binde
> *If I lose my life, I bind fast*
> swearte Wealas,    hwilum sellan men.
> *dark Welshmen, sometimes better men.*
> Hwilum Ic deorum    drincan selle
> *Sometimes I give a brave warrior drink*
> beorne of bosme;    hwilum mec bryd triedeð
> *from my breast; sometimes a stately bride treads*
> felawlonc fotum;    hwilum feorran broht
> *her foot on me; sometimes, brought far from Wales,*
> wonfeax Wale    wegeð ond þyð,
> *a dark-haired Welsh woman shakes and presses me;*
> dol druncmennen,    deorcum nihtum,
> *some stupid, drunken slave-girl, on dark nights*

wæteð in wætre,    wyrmeð hwilum

*wets me in water, she warms me pleasantly*

fægre to fyre;    me on fæðme sticaþ

*for a while by the fire; a lustful hand grabs me*

hygegalan hond,    hwyrfeð geneahhe,

*in an embrace, and moves me about frequently,*

swifeð me geond sweartne.    Saga hwæt Ic hatte

*then sweeps me through that blackness. Say what I am called,*

þe Ic lifgende    lond reafige,

*I who living ravage the land,*

ond æfter deaþe    dryhtum þeowige.

*and after death serve the elite multitudes.*

This riddle is deliberately full of sexual innuendo and double entendre, which presumably titillated, entertained, and taught the reader-listener the art of seeing multiple meanings in words and phrases. The subject of the poem reveals it is about a once-living thing that now serves to restrain Welsh slaves; as a container for drink; or as a hot-water bottle, filled by a Welsh slave girl; or as a brush for her dark hair. While alive (and free, in contrast to the slaves), the riddle-subject is an ox; after death, it serves the multitudes as leather or ox-hide, the most flexible of products. So integrated into the social life of the early Middle Ages was servitude, though, that slaves of both sexes are casually inserted into a riddlic game centred on the multiple potential uses of disguised objects.

Contact and cultural exchange between Celts and Anglo-Saxons continued (King Alfred's 9th-century adviser and biographer was Asser, the Welsh bishop of St David's in Wales, for example), though it is complex and often difficult to trace. Something of the complexity can be discerned from extant literary texts, which are predominantly written in Latin in the earliest centuries after the arrival of the Anglo-Saxons, though literature in all languages will also have been transmitted orally.

## On origins

For Gildas, the arrival of the Anglo-Saxons was catastrophic. If the relative unimportance of Celtic languages in the development of English and the casual mention of enslaved Welsh is convincing evidence, the Anglo-Saxon 'settlement' was, indeed, a catastrophe for the subordinated peoples. For the prolific author Bede (673–735), a monk-priest writing in 8th-century northeast England at the monastery of Wearmouth-Jarrow, one people's crisis was another's opportunity. From his *Historia ecclesiastica gentis Anglorum* (*Ecclesiastical History of the English People*), completed in 731, we discover most of what there is to learn about the early centuries of British history. Bede provides an account of the arrival of the Anglo-Saxons, and the foundation of England up to his time, helping to provide an idea of what constituted Englishness. The *Ecclesiastical History* was influential immediately, and considered by King Alfred to be among 'the books most necessary for all men to know'. It was translated from Latin into Old English in the late 9th or early 10th century, and copied many times thereafter.

Numerous significant events are marked in the course of this substantial work, and none is of greater canonical status than Bede's narration of the arrival of the Anglo-Saxons at the request of Vortigern, echoing Gildas in aspects of the story. With geographical specificity (see Figure 1) and the pinpointing of person by name and descent, Bede comments in Book 1, Chapter xv (here from the Old English version) that:

> They came from among the three most powerful Germanic tribes, those of the Saxons, the Angles and the Jutes. The people in Kent and in the Isle of Wight are of Jutish origin. From the Saxons, that is from that land which is called Saxony, come those in Essex, Sussex, and Wessex. And from the Angles come the East Anglians and Middle Anglians and Mercians and all the people of

Northumbria. That land which is called Angeln is between Jutland and Saxony. It is said that from the time they left there until the present day that it remains deserted. The first of their leaders and commanders were two brothers, Hengest and Horsa. They were the sons of Wihtgysl, whose father was called Wihta, this Wihta's father was named Woden, from whose lineage many tribes of royal races claimed their origin.

Bede also describes the destruction that was heaped by the Anglo-Saxons, 'with the righteous judgement of God', upon the island's Celtic inhabitants, the 'graceless people', in collaboration with the Pictish tribes in the far north. This critically important work establishes the major account of the earliest foundation of the English nation in an authorial act that deliberately unites the peoples of England into one nation under God and the Roman church.

This focus was especially important during the decades in which Bede lived and practised his religious life. In 597, St Augustine was sent by Pope Gregory the Great to convert the pagan Angles and Saxons in the south of England, who, prior to conversion, worshipped the pantheon of northern gods. Yet, at the same time as those in Kent, Sussex, Wessex, and East Anglia were gradually becoming Christian, another branch of Christianity was already firmly rooted in the west and north, brought from Ireland via the holy island of Iona. This Celtic Christianity competed with the Roman version during the 7th century, to be settled in favour of the Roman tradition at the Synod of Whitby in 664.

Celtic traditions, reconciled with the Roman, were exemplified in the single person of the Lindisfarne hermit, St Cuthbert. Although he had been raised to practise Celtic Christianity, he was present when the English church chose Roman Christianity at Whitby. Bede wrote about Cuthbert's pious and ascetic life in Book IV of the *Ecclesiastical History*. Bede had also written a pair of biographies focused on Cuthbert before this—'both in heroic verse and also in prose'. These saintly biographies, or hagiographies, were among the most prolific genres of the medieval period, and they often drew on earlier stories growing in length and complexity as the text was transmitted through the centuries.

Such was the fame of both Bede and Cuthbert that their intertwined histories continue to be well known throughout the centuries since. Bede, as one of the Church Fathers, was the only named Englishman in Dante's early 14th-century Italian epic, *The Divine Comedy* (in *Paradiso*, Canto X); and Cuthbert still remains the patron saint of northern England. He is interred at Durham Cathedral close to Bede, and it was during the translation of Cuthbert's remains at Durham in 1104 that his grave was found to contain a number of artefacts associated with him that survive to this day. Among these finds is the 'literature' that would have been a permanent part of Cuthbert's life, the sacred words of the Gospel of John, a manuscript of which was found at the head of Cuthbert's body when he was translated. This small hand-sized book, written in Latin in the late 7th century, is now known as 'The St Cuthbert Gospel' and it is the earliest Western book still in its original binding. Bought by the British Library in 2012 from its former owners for £7,000,000, the little book, fully digitized for all to see on the British Library's website, attests to the significance of the early Anglo-Saxons' spiritual, literary, and cultural legacy.

## Mixing traditions

As well as this early Latin written tradition, a great many texts in the medieval period—especially vernacular poetic works—were often not copied down for years, sometimes centuries, after their initial composition. These include works in Celtic languages other than Welsh and Irish, like Pictish and Scottish Gaelic (perhaps derived from Irish Gaelic), or poems and stories in Old Norse—the other major Germanic language in the British Isles after the late 9th century. As such, our idea of literary production is skewed by what survives in the record, and the date of a manuscript's text may not correlate at all with the date of a work's composition and initial transmission. Sometimes, only whispers of dynamic earlier literary traditions can be traced through the written texts.

A notable example of a vernacular textual remnant is undoubtedly *Cædmon's Hymn*, the survival of which we owe to scribes writing in a context very close to Bede's own. Students who learn Old English Literature (see Box 3) at university level will certainly encounter this short poem. Within a very short time around the year of Bede's death in 735, scribes copied two Latin manuscripts

## Box 3 Old English literature

'Old English' is the name given to the language and the literature of the Anglo-Saxons, peoples who, from their Germanic origins in northern Europe, settled the area roughly the same as modern-day England from about 450 CE. Anglo-Saxon England lasted up to the Norman Conquest in about 1066, but Old English literature continued to be produced and used into the early 13th century.

Hundreds of manuscripts containing Old English survive, principally from the 9th century onwards, when King Alfred of Wessex (d. 899) initiated a major educational reform that resulted in the writing of Old English. Old English comprised the West Saxon, Northumbrian, Anglian, Mercian, and Kentish dialects; but most surviving texts are written in West Saxon. The range of works is astonishing: from religious and secular poems to sermons and saints' lives, historical, medical, legal, and didactic prose. Most of what remains is anonymous, though a few authors' names are known, such as Cynewulf, Alfred, Ælfric, Byrhtferth, and Wulfstan. Four main books containing the majority of Old English alliterative verse exist (the *Beowulf*-manuscript, the Exeter Book, the Junius Manuscript, and the Vercelli Book), and poetry constitutes 10 per cent of the overall corpus.

of the *Ecclesiastical History*. In the Moore Bede (Cambridge, University Library, Kk. 5. 16) and the St Petersburg Bede (Saint Petersburg, National Library of Russia, lat. Q. v. I. 18), scribes working on these books added the Old English version of the poem sung by Cædmon as recorded in Latin in the Bede narrative. Bede tells us that a cowherd at the monastery of Whitby in the modern-day county of Yorkshire was at a drinking-party with his friends when the harp approached him, being passed around for partygoers to use to create poetry that would thus be musically accompanied. Cædmon the cowherd left the party, embarrassed because he could not sing the extemporary poetic-songs beloved of the Anglo-Saxons and other northern European peoples. Cædmon went back to his shed to tend to his animals and fell asleep, only to have a vision of an angel, who demanded that he sing something ('Cædmon, sing me hwæthwugu'):

'Ne con Ic noht singan; ond Ic for þon of þeossum gebeorscipe ut eode, ond hider gewat, for þon Ic naht singan ne cuðe.' Eft he cwæð, se ðe wið hine sprecende wæs: 'Hwæðre þu me aht singan.' Þa cwæð he, 'Hwæt sceal Ic singan?' Cwæð he: 'Sing me frumsceaft.'

*'I'm not able to sing anything; and because of that, I went out of the beer-party, and came here, because I don't know how to sing anything'. Again [the angel] spoke, he who was talking with him: 'Nevertheless, you can sing something for me.' Then he said, 'What shall I sing?' He said: 'Sing to me about the creation.'*

This rather charmingly told exchange between Cædmon and the visiting angel sets the scene for the earliest surviving Christian poem in English, miraculously uttered by a new talent who was subsequently made famous throughout the community. And while the poem that Cædmon sang was incorporated by Bede into his *Ecclesiastical History* in Latin, those contemporary scribes who imported the vernacular versions clearly felt it essential to have the original rendition present within the story.

So it is that at the apposite point in the narrative, at folio 107 recto of the St Petersburg Bede, one of the manuscript's scribes wrote the poem in Northumbrian dialect in the lower margin. When it is laid out as verse in the way that modern editors prefer, it reads:

Nu scilun herga hefenricæs Uard,
*Now we should praise the heavenly kingdom's Guardian,*
Metudæs mehti and his modgithanc,
*the Measurer's might and his conception,*
uerc Uuldurfadur, sue he uundra gihuæs,
*the work of the glorious Father, as he for every wonder,*
eci Dryctin, or astelidæ.
*eternal Lord, established a beginning.*
He ærist scop aeldu barnum
*He first shaped for sons of men*
hefen to hrofæ, halig Sceppend;
*heaven as a roof, holy Creator;*
tha middingard moncynnæs Uard,
*then middle-earth, mankind's Guardian,*
eci Dryctin, æfter tiadæ
*eternal Lord, afterwards adorned,*
firum foldu, Frea allmehtig.
*the earth for men, Lord almighty.*

This poem is without parallel in terms of its significance as the beginning of canonical English literature. Cædmon's miraculous outpouring of praise for God's creation effectively and evocatively melds two quite disparate traditions in a way that provided a precedent for the majority of English poetry written up to the end of the Anglo-Saxon period, and intermittently thereafter. It is fitting that the combination of Christian, and not pagan Germanic, theme and Germanic alliterative verse-form emerges in a paean to God. This is reminiscent of the Latin hymns beloved of the early Irish missionaries, like Columbanus (543–615), who founded monasteries on the European mainland, and Columba (521–97), who founded the monastery at Iona, in Scotland.

In Cædmon's verse, the alliterative-accentual form, typical of Germanic verse and rhythmically mimicking the patterns of natural speech, is adapted for Christian purposes for the first time. The alliteration binding the stressed syllables of the first and second half-lines permits key words to be heavily emphasized; in the first three lines, for instance, the alliterating syllables are those nouns and adjectives beginning with <h>, <m>, and <u> (pronounced as <w>). The demands of alliteration are such that multiple synonyms or near-synonyms are required for the principal persons or ideas. Here, God is 'guardian', 'creator', 'father', 'lord'; he is 'mighty', 'eternal', 'holy', and 'almighty'.

Structure is given to the sequence by main words providing the 'head stave' at the first stressed syllable of the second half-line: *hefenricæs* ('of the heavenly kingdom'), *modgithanc* ('conception'), *uundra* ('of the wonders'), *or* ('beginning') and this word is the most emphatic of all. The caesura in the middle of the verse-line creates a dramatic pause, but the pause—shown as a space in modern editions of this poetry—never occurs as an actual space in the manuscripts themselves; instead, all early English poetry is laid out in the manuscript as if it were prose. But this slight pause in the verse-line's delivery is ideal for oral performance, as Cædmon proved the day after his nighttime vision, when he sang the Creation song for the wise monks at the abbey of Whitby. In this and later performances as a singer of religious verse, Cædmon gained fame sufficient to be enshrined in Bede's national history, thereby providing an originary legend for the significant corpus of vernacular poetry that emerged in the centuries following.

# Chapter 2
# Textual production and performance

Unlike modern mass-produced books and documents printed on machine-made paper, each medieval book or document or note is unique, hand-made, and handwritten by a scribe with a feather-quill or reed pen and ink. Practice versions of texts or preliminary work might be inscribed with a stylus into a wax tablet, which could then be heated, smoothed and used again, or copied quickly onto scraps of membrane. Final versions of a text were usually the careful products of those who had been trained to write formally by teachers, who would most often be monks, priests, or nuns. Children and novices would be taught in ecclesiastical schools or aristocratic households. In the later centuries, secular schools emerged to teach those who already had sufficient social standing to attain an education. All the books and documents produced by those with training in writing were prepared in similar ways.

From around the 1st century BCE, animal skin (and in the Mediterranean, papyrus) was used as the main substrate for textual production, though inscribed objects and large carved memorials exist too, ranging from stone crosses, to ivory combs, wooden tally sticks, embellished book-covers, woven textiles, and many other artefacts. Books and documents, though, were generally made from parchment (sheepskin), vellum (calfskin), or goatskin. It was a complicated, costly, and time-consuming job to manufacture skins for writing, but this in itself reveals a great deal about how valued textual production and curation was. Throughout the medieval period in the British Isles, and up until the 14th century when hand-made paper began to be increasingly employed in writing environments, books and documents were written on skin by highly trained scribes, to be read by the privileged literate elite. But as the centuries passed, those numbers of readers and writers grew significantly, and with that growth came a much greater demand for texts and books, increasing the scale of manufacture, changing the modes of production, and effecting new means of dissemination.

## Making books

As is clear from looking at the earliest works that survive from the medieval British Isles, the majority of texts produced were religious or legal in nature. When Christianity arrived in the south of England in the last years of the 6th century, the missionaries probably brought with them books from Rome that would be used to preach conversion. Thereafter, sermons, the Gospels, and instructional and teaching texts were all essential in the spread of the new religion and were produced by religious scribes in writing offices known as scriptoria. These varied in size, depending on the institution's wealth and population. The scribes regarded their work as part of their *opus Dei*, 'God's work'. This could be quite physical and arduous in the depths of a chilly winter, when scribes sat writing in drafty carrels, struggling to see their exemplar in the dimming light, as they wrote biblical and didactic works to venerate God.

From the very late 6th and 7th centuries, for example, a number of books influenced by Celtic Christianity survive. The Cathach of St Columba, though damaged, contains beautiful decorated initial capitals surrounded by red dots, an archetypal Celtic motif, seen also in other Celtic-inspired manuscripts. This Cathach, a

Psalter or Book of Psalms, hung around the neck of a holy man and was used apotropaically; that is, to bless and seek protection for fighting forces before a battle. The Book of Durrow, written perhaps at Iona or in Northumbria in the 7th century, is the oldest complete gospel-book from the British Isles, and, like the few other famous books of the 7th and 8th centuries, it shows great influence from the Celtic tradition of illustration and decoration.

Monastic and other ecclesiastical institutions manufactured medieval books until at least the 12th century, and among the most highly venerated manuscripts to survive from the medieval period are the oldest, like London, British Library, Cotton Nero D. iv, known as the Lindisfarne Gospels. This large book was produced in early 8th-century Northumbria, and is fully digitized on the British Library's website. Written by the scribe Eadfrith, the Gospels were richly illuminated in gold and coloured inks made from precious materials. Carpet-pages filled with geometrical decoration face the first folio of each Gospel, to create extraordinarily complex and visually demanding openings. A manuscript like the Lindisfarne Gospels was expensive and resource heavy, and the value of the book was deeply felt even at that time by the community of monks that produced it. When the monks fled from the Vikings' attacks on Lindisfarne, they took the book, as one of their treasures, with them.

Gospel-books, and other major liturgical works, often belonged to the institution rather than a particular individual, and became showpieces for the religious establishments that made them. In the 12th century, very large, elaborately illuminated bibles were manufactured at great expense in what might be regarded as the apogee of book production within the monastic tradition. Sometimes, these may have been dedicated to wealthy patrons, or brought out on display in the church and shown to noble visitors to impress them. At this time, too, the production of some books became the responsibility of professional scribes and artists, like the famous 12th-century artist Master Hugo, who travelled between institutions to make a living in the expert manufacture of books.

Thousands of other books and documents were made besides these highly decorated, expensive volumes, typically made by wealthy institutions and nowadays seen in exhibitions in manuscript repositories around the world. The 'average' manuscript—as if any handmade object can be 'average'—is a portable, plain artefact, containing texts that were essential for the needs of the user or owner. Ownership of books was restricted either to those who belonged to religious communities, or to those in noble households, or, by the 13th century, to students who attended the newly instituted universities of Oxford and Cambridge, who were often engaged in a religious life themselves. At this time, too, book production methods changed with many books becoming smaller, as handwriting became more compressed and the page layout changed. This made the production of books cheaper and more commercially viable. With the book becoming a commodity for wider audiences, writing shops came into existence to cater for the much greater demand for texts.

## Textual communities

Traceable textual communities in the earlier Middle Ages tended to be dominated by religious communities of monks, nuns, and canons and those who were their congregations. Some form of literacy was expected of people in holy orders, since they were needed to pray, to practise pastoral care for those souls in their charge, and to be the producers of the books needed for the promulgation of a learned, Christian message. This remained true throughout the medieval period. But, as the centuries progressed noble secular households, including first and foremost the king's court, became important patrons of and audiences for literature, often fostering an elite literate culture, and helping to establish new forms of textual production.

In the post-Conquest period, after about 1100, French literature (see Box 4) began to be produced in England, partly as a result of the precedent of a long English vernacular tradition, and partly as a result of the keen literary interests of aristocratic and religious women. Henry I's second wife, Adeliza of Louvain, was a keen patron of literature: she was the dedicatee of one of the earliest French texts written in England in the first quarter of the 12th century, Benedeit's *Le Voyage de Saint Brendan*,

---

## Box 4  French literature

Inspired perhaps by the long-standing literary tradition they discovered in England, the Normans who conquered in 1066 began to produce works in their own language from about c.1100. This vibrant corpus of literature is also known as Anglo-Norman, or insular French, or French of England, and it differs from continental French in having its own traditions and trends. Saints' lives and histories predominated in the first part of the 12th century, but from the second half of the century, romances, lyrics, and lays proliferated.

From the 13th century until at least the 15th, there is an astonishingly innovative and varied corpus of prose, poetic, and dramatic texts written in French. Since French was the language of the monarchy, aristocracy, government, law, some clerical institutions, and scholarship, it had a major impact on the trajectory of British and Irish literature and culture. Its importance is seen in the very large number of French words taken into English between the 12th and the later 14th centuries.

After the 15th century, English began to displace French as the language of literary production in England, though French maintained its prestige. The relationship between the various languages and their late medieval written traditions is only now becoming clear with new research generating an appreciation for the importance of French.

a poem in octosyllabic rhyming couplets (eight-syllable pairs of lines). The narrative was based on Latin legends of the 6th-century Irish saint, which told the story of his journeys and encounters with extraordinary creatures, people, and places, including a glimpse of heaven.

The empress Matilda, daughter of Henry I and mother of Henry II, was keen to foster literature in the 12th century, too, as was Eleanor of Aquitaine, wife of Henry II, and one of the most important figures in the cultural renaissance of the 12th century. Eleanor patronized Wace, the author of the French *Roman de Rou*, the *Brut*, and the verse lives of Saints Nicholas and Margaret. Constance, the wife of the Lincolnshire lord Ralf Fitzgilbert, was the patron of the French *Estoire des Engleis*, written by Geoffrey Gaimar in the mid-12th century. This *Estoire* was the first translation into the vernacular of Geoffrey of Monmouth's famous *Historia regum Britanniae* (*History of the Kings of Britain*), completed in 1137. Evidence suggests a female interest in historiography and especially the history of Britain and its royal lineage, together with romance in its earliest phases.

In the later centuries, textual communities became more varied still. From university students to professional householders, as literacy became more widespread, so owners and users of books diversified. The main producer and first owner of the 13th-century multilingual manuscript, Oxford, Bodleian Library, Digby 86, was a secular educated man who lived in the west of England. He copied most of the manuscript over a period of time, aiming to include literary and religious works, predominantly in French, that he might have read to his entire household. Thus, as was so often the case, one book probably had a large audience, who would have participated communally through listening, rather than through direct and personal reading.

Throughout rural communities and towns, one important form of literacy was not necessarily highly expert; rather, it was 'functional' or pragmatic. Tradespeople and those with some rudimentary education knew enough to get by and might have been able to write their name, or understand significant phrases. These textual communities grew in number and in proficiency by the end of the Middle Ages, paralleling the emergence of a large and productive middle class. Evidence for this kind of literacy comes from many texts, including Chaucer's late 14th-century *Canterbury Tales*. This engaging and animated work depicts a diverse group of fictional pilgrims each of whom is meant to tell a story to the other assembled characters as they make their way to Canterbury on their pilgrimage. Among these figures are the Summoner, a minor cleric, who can parrot Latin phrases; a Reeve, who manages his lord's estates; and other professional characters including the Guildsmen, the Wife of Bath, and the Merchant all of whom would have some access to texts, even if, like the Wife of Bath, they were not that proficient as readers themselves.

## Composing and performing

As well as accessing texts through reading, medieval textual communities functioned without tangible books. These were oral or auditory cultures; that is, audiences who participated in the telling of tales and singing of songs through performance, or who heard the narration of secular literature and religious messages in different kinds of environments through the words of poets and preachers, storytellers and teachers. Many labels exist to describe the oral performers of a particular medieval cultural group: *scops* and bards were the early tellers of tales for the Anglo-Saxons and the Celts; skalds were the poets of the Old Norse traditions. By the 12th century, the French troubadours and trouvères travelled through European courts and noble households singing the love lyrics and *lais* that played such a major role in literary composition in the late Middle Ages. Later, in the 14th and 15th centuries, highly organized and collaborative dramatic performers emerged onto the streets of the city or village, filling the open spaces with spectacle and noise.

Within the oral and auditory community, one text or one image could have far greater impact than can be measured by surviving instances of that text. Or, single surviving texts, like the single early Welsh riddlic text, *Kat Godeu*, 'The Battle of the Trees', from the *Llyfr Taliesin (Book of Taliesin)*, attest to what might have been a much more prolific literary tradition. Moreover, with performance, the transient mode of delivery to a crowd that is live and present, but then disperses, often leaves no physical trace of its happening. This appears to be the way in which early textual traditions functioned in all societies: through oral dissemination of a text only much later recorded in writing.

In the case of the early medieval British bard, Taliesin, poems attributed to his authorship date from the late 6th century, but are not found in manuscript form until the 14th century, when they were copied into the *Llyfr Taliesin* (Aberystwyth, National Library of Wales, Peniarth 2, which is fully digitized on the National Library's website). Quite what the 'original' compositions of this bard and his fellow British poets (known as *Y Cynfeirdd*) were really like is impossible to deduce and 'authorship' becomes an impossibly difficult concept to prove. In the form in which they survive, these poems concern themselves with the heroic ethos in which they were culturally situated, but they clearly also speak to the 14th-century audience that produced and received these works. In *Gwaith Argoed Llwyfain (The Affair of Argoed Llwyfain)*, Taliesin writes in praise of the British king Urien Rheged and his son Owain, 'the wounder of the east', relating their battle victories:

> Atorelwis Uryen vd yr echwyd,
> *Then Urien, the lord of Yrechwydd, shouted out,*
> 'O byd ymgyfaruot am gerenhyd
> *'If there's to be gathering to talk of peace,*
> dyrchafwn eidoed oduch mynyd
> *let us raise our banners on the mountain*

> ac am porthwn wyneb oduch emyl.
> *and raise our faces above the shield's edge.*
> A dyrchafwn peleidyr oduch pen gwyr
> *Let us raise spears above men's heads*
> a chyrchwn fflamdwyn yny luyd
> *and fall on Fflamddwyn among his hosts*
> a lladwn ac ef ae gyweithyd!'
> *and kill both him and his company!'*

This rousing speech, which apparently took place in battle during the later 6th century, is clearly a poetic affirmation—rich in rhyme and alliteration—of Urien's warrior prowess and leadership over his men. In Taliesin's poem, Urien's speech insists on the literal and metaphorical rising up of his men and their weapons in order to crush the enemy from a moral and physical height. Taliesin proclaims that until the day he dies he will praise Urien, and such ancient eulogy, known as *hengerdd* in the Welsh tradition, survives in all the Celtic and Germanic cultures in the medieval period. Professional poets from the earliest to the latest time in medieval society were paid by patrons to regale the whole community with skilful narrations of war-deeds, the better to encourage the listeners in their resolve and desire for victory. They were deeply knowledgeable about history, poetic formulas, and style, and about communities, their ancestry, and their affiliations.

Similarly, then, legend and the careful remembrance of national narratives going back for generations played a major part in the survival and transmission of the great Irish prose saga, the *Táin Bó Cúailnge* (*The Cattle Raid of Cooley*), which survives in manuscripts from the 12th century, though its historical context is perhaps a millennium earlier. These early texts, in both poetry and prose, survive principally because they were passed from teller to teller, evolving and transforming as they continued to entertain and teach. This method of dissemination and the communal understanding that texts were not *fixed*, as they tend to seem through print, means that medieval literature can be thought of as part of a fluid, changing, and dynamic process. This is true whether one or more versions of a work exist in written form. And because texts were regarded as still-living and authors were often not known, many scribes became part of the authorial process, editing texts both deliberately and inadvertently as they effectively created new versions of the words they had received from an exemplar.

This shifting literary culture seen in Welsh and Irish literary production is also witnessed in all other literary contexts in the Middle Ages. In terms of manuscript variation, a most dramatic example is Chaucer's *Canterbury Tales*, which exists in over eighty unique manuscripts and fragments, dating from *c.*1400 onwards. None of these versions is the same as any other and, indeed, some of the variations between the manuscripts' texts and sequences of texts are very notable. Since not one manuscript is written by Chaucer himself, scholars of the *Tales* research how close to Chaucer's authorial intentions the texts in these manuscripts might be, and how much scribe-editors influenced the production of their respective versions. The same issues of 'who wrote the manuscript' and 'how close is the text to authorial intention' affect many texts, including those that exist in only one manuscript. With the Arthurian romance *Sir Gawain and the Green Knight*, for example, no one knows who the author of the poem was, or when or how it was written. Later literary categories of 'originality', 'date of composition', 'authoritative text', and 'authorship' are thus more complex for medieval literature, but, interestingly, such openness gives readers a great deal of interpretative flexibility, too.

## Textual settings

Just as the circumstances surrounding the 'origin' of a literary work are very murky, either because no 'original' exists and the author is unknown, or because we do not know where or when a work's life began, so, too, the environments in which texts were accessed are often unclear. It is likely that medieval communal audiences were privy to public performances of heroic works and romances, mythical tale-tellings, magnificent oral recitations, and spiritual declamations that lived on in the mind and collective memory.

In the mead-hall of Germanic society, which lasted well into the 11th century in England, or the courtly hall of the regional nobleman, audiences gathered over a meal to be entertained and inspired by works like, respectively, the satirical 12th- or 13th-century Welsh prose *Breuddwyd Rhonabwy* (*The Dream of Rhonabwy*), or the 15th-century romance, *The Awyntyrs of Arthure* (*Adventures of Arthur*). Some literary works contain a self-representational moment, where their own origins are declaimed. *Widsith*, an Old English fragmentary verse about the poet whose name means 'far-journey', begins with the narration of himself in the third person which illustrates the reception he can expect from listeners in the lord's hall, who would reward him with treasure and patronage:

> Widsith spoke, unlocked his word-hoard,
> he who had travelled most of all men
> through tribes and nations across the earth
> had often gained great treasure in hall.

Widsith's story is a good reminder of the importance of the social gathering as the place of critical information exchange and communal recollection.

The gathering of the community to hear texts read aloud continued into the modern era, particularly because books were expensive and relatively rare and because levels of literacy ranged variously from exceptionally low to only partial to accomplished until the mandatory education of children in the 19th century. A picture of Geoffrey Chaucer on the first folio of a 15th-century manuscript, Cambridge, Corpus Christi College 61 (see Figure 3),

3. Cambridge, Corpus Christi College 61, folio 1 verso.

shows him reading his great romance, *Troilus and Criseyde*, from a raised dais to King Richard II and an assembly of some two or three dozen courtiers. Obviously, in all performance circumstances like this, some would hear or see better than others, depending on seating or vantage point. In the case of medieval dramas like the York Corpus Christi Plays, or the Chester Mystery Plays performed in the streets from at least the 15th century, if not earlier (and, for the last few decades, performed live in the streets of these modern cities once more), audience participation matters for the plays' literal, social, and spiritual success. From this physical and real-time participation in re-enacted moments of Christ's life, the opportunity for a personal engagement with the key episodes in New Testament history are obviously a critical element of the event and it is to the reader's responses that Chapter 3 will turn.

# Chapter 3
# Literary spaces, literary identities

## Reading and hearing

In contrast to the hurly-burly of the pageant wagons in the medieval street plays, in the 21st century we might tend initially to think of accessing a text as a solitary experience, even though many public stagings of texts still occur (like cinema-goers' experiences, for instance). In the Middle Ages, textual access could also include the effort of an individual reader, who might generally have articulated the words of the text out loud. This seems to have been the norm for the solo reader.

Nevertheless, the audience of a text—whether private or public, silent or noisy—is asked to engage with that text, to identify with or mull over the contents of the work. This is not to suggest that all textual participants have the *same* experience, even in the setting of a single public performance. Any individual's reception of a text depends on many different factors including their position in the audience, or the audibility of speaker, and the knowledge, understanding, and concentration that the listener-viewer brings to bear on the experience. Authors also employ particular tactics to encourage the formation of a collective response and build a common frame of reference. The opening lines of the Old English epic poem *Beowulf*, written down in *c.*1010 (in the manuscript London, British Library, Cotton

Vitellius A. xv), insist on a pre-existing body of shared knowledge among the imagined audience:

> Hwæt, we Gardena in geardagum,
> *Listen, we heard of the Spear-Danes in olden days,*
> þeodcyninga þrym gefrunon,
> *of the glory of the people's kings,*
> hu ða æþelingas ellen fremedon.
> *how the princes performed courageous deeds.*

In this opening to the poem, the performer (perhaps in dramatic mode in the hall of a noble person) encourages unity among his listeners by the use of the pronoun 'we' and the claim that everyone has 'heard' about the Spear-Danes already; everyone shares these events in tribal history and legend. In its 3,182 lines, the poem creates a world that focuses on three major encounters between Beowulf and ferocious monsters. The ethos that pervades the poem, both in the choice of vocabulary and in the narrative it constructs, is the Germanic Heroic Code of loyalty, bravery, heroism, and the giving and receiving of treasure by lord and thane (or warrior). These opening lines establish this code, anticipating the potential audience's participation. All of this is effectively implied by 'we'.

Beyond *Beowulf* and other works about the heroic individual's role in society, it is also very common to encounter the rhetoric of inclusion when the author seeks to bring the intended audience into the text. Authors will seek agreement to win the reader or audience member over, and perhaps win promotion, acclaim, or patronage at the same time. In this, the success of a text was partly dependent on the space of performance: the appropriateness of the venue mattered. The ambience of a provincial lord's hall might have made the dramatic rehearsal of battle-song a moment of group glory; or conversely, an elegy, lamenting the loss of a recently deceased person, could inspire some truly moving moments for the individual or group.

Geoffrey Chaucer's elegiac *Book of the Duchess* was written in or just after 1369, for Henry III's son, John of Gaunt. It commemorates John's young wife, Blanche, who had died of the plague, though the cause is not mentioned in this formal poem. Notably, this work comes at a critical moment in the history of literary production in England, as Chaucer chose very deliberately to write his first major poem for the royal court in English, not French, which had been the language of prestige and status since the late 11th century. While the poem is a public statement of sorrow, read to an assembled group of sympathetic nobles, it is also moving and delicate, drawing inspiration from earlier writers, like the classical Latin author, Ovid, and Chaucer's contemporary, Guillaume de Machaut, a French poet.

In *The Book of the Duchess*, Chaucer maintains the balance between courtly decorum and personal elegy by casting the poem as a dream vision, in which the poet meets and converses with the mournful Black Knight (representing John of Gaunt), who reveals the death of his 'lady swete, | That was so fair, so fresh, so fre'. Through the remembrance of falling in love, and the articulation of Blanche's sweetness and nobility, the poem becomes a celebration of love, a small consolation for substantial loss, presumably delivered within the courtly context where Blanche was most well known.

A much earlier eulogistic poem praising the achievements of a well-known figure is the early and lengthy Irish *Elegy for St Columba* (*Amra Choluim Chille*), composed by St Dallan in the 6th century, though it only survives in manuscripts from the 12th century. It was read out to an assembly of Irish lords, which we learn from the author's declaration about his motivation: that he wishes to attain heaven through the work's public performance, and hopes, too, to promote the patronage of poets in Ireland (see Box 5). This poem is partly self-reflexive, calling attention to its own performative wonder by lauding the miraculous voice of the saint that could resound far and wide:

Son a gotha Coluim Cille
*The sound of Colum Cille's voice,*
mór a binne húas cech cléir:
*great was its sweetness above every company:*
co cend cóic cét déc céimmend
*as far away as fifteen hundred paces,*
aidblib réimmend ed ba réil.
*a vastness of courses, it was clear.*

Rather like the story of Cædmon the cowherd, whose sudden ability to sing was a sign of God's grace, the story of Columba's

## Box 5  Irish literature

Irish literature in the native language and in Latin flourished from very early in the period: Ogham inscriptions survive; and Christian legends were transmitted into manuscripts from the 8th century, attesting to the highly literate culture of the Irish. Irish influence extended far beyond the island, because of Christian missionaries on the European continent and in northern and western Britain. Poetry and prose in Irish survive in quantity from the 12th century onwards, and a good deal of the material written down in the High Middle Ages can be dated earlier, giving important evidence for the foundational stories of the Irish kingdoms. These include the great cycles of legendary and mythological texts like the *Cycles of the Kings* and the *Fenian Cycle*.

A notable piece of Irish literature is the poem *Pangur Bán*, written in the 9th century by an Irish monk while he was in Reichenau Abbey in south Germany. The poet addresses his cat, Pangur Bán, praising the cat's skill at catching mice and relating that skill to his own as a scribe, who turns 'darkness into light' through his work. This humorous poem highlights something of the diversity of Irish literature, with its substantial sustained corpus of Christian and secular poetry and prose.

resounding voice told to an appreciative audience of nobles could hardly disadvantage the skilful poet. That *this* is the miracle, too—the capacity for the saint's voice to be heard so widely—suggests the importance of oral dissemination to medieval culture throughout Britain and Ireland, the significance of the message being heard.

But, more privately, the witticisms and stylistic complexity of a Latin verse satirizing the church might most profitably be transmitted to a group of trained and educated persons in the scholarly setting of the university or a monastic institution. One such set of texts, which are 'goliardic' (belonging to the genre of satirical poems aimed against the church, and written in the 12th and 13th centuries by itinerant scholars), exists in a manuscript anthology that probably belonged to a Benedictine monk, William of Winchester, in the 13th century—London, British Library, Harley 978 (fully digitized on the British Library website). Other literary works in this manuscript include a hunting tract, medical treatises, and the music and lyrics for a Middle English song, *Sumer is icumen in*, with its Latin counterpart, *Perspice, Christicola* ('See, O Christ').

The manuscript also contains the important French *Lais* and *Fables* of Marie de France, an author living and writing in England in the later 12th century. The *Lais*, dedicated by Marie to Henry II (d. 1189) are short Arthurian narratives about chivalric love—that is, the love of knights and their ladies, containing thematic conventions such as loyalty and betrayal, disguise and revelation, and the intervention of supernatural elements. Stories of these events, or *aventures*, were originally composed and performed musically by Breton minstrels. Marie's intention in putting together these *Lais*, such as *Lanval*, *Yonec*, and *Chevrefoil*, as she declares in her Prologue, was to bring life to these ancient tales. Within this single manuscript context, then, while the diverse collection of entertaining, didactic, and instructive works suggest the book was specifically made for the interests of its individual owner or primary user, a number of texts seem to demand public and even courtly performance, indicating a multitude of possible contexts of textual delivery.

## Capturing audiences, creating history

In the wonderfully entertaining and deeply humorous late 12th-century work, *De nugis curialium* (*Trifles of Courtiers*), Walter Map (d. 1209/10) regales his audience of like-minded male clerics at court with a treasure-trove of legend, historical narrative, and contemporary detail that represents the wide range of knowledge an educated person could acquire. Map was a well-connected churchman from the Marches of Wales, who studied at Paris and rose to become archdeacon of Oxford. His intention in writing *De nugis* was apparently to inspire and inform. He likens the assiduous reader, the 'lover of wisdom', to a busy bee that draws something from everything it lands upon. But not so the ungodly:

> non sic: sed oderunt antequam audierint, vilipendunt antequam appendant, ut sicut in sordibus sunt sordescat adhuc. Solum ex hoc placeo quod vetusta loquor. Libetne tamen nuper actis aurem dare parumper?

> *not so: they hate before they have heard; they disparage before they deliberate, so that as they are filthy, they become filthier still. The only merit is that I tell of ancient things. Will you please, though, for a little while, give ear to a story of recent times?*

By humorously derogating the ignorant, ungodly person, whose lack of willingness to learn is likened to being filthy, Map forms a desire in his audience to be more akin to the busy learner. In this request for his listener or reader to pay attention for a little longer, Map deftly creates a respondent who can only say 'yes', if *they* wish to be among the pursuers of wisdom. Such rhetoric consolidates the relationship between writer and listener-reader, a rhetoric that wittily sought the audience's approval and compliance, a rhetoric that persuaded.

To a greater or lesser extent, all literature seeks to engage, inform, and persuade. In order to engage an audience, a literary work has to grab the audience's attention and reveal something worth hearing. Literature can play a significant role in shaping an audience's thoughts, ideas, and sense of itself, and throughout the Middle Ages among the most important genres was the chronicle or history. This form of writing was important from the early medieval period onwards, as exemplified by the Latin histories of Gildas or Bede, for example. Histories help to promote a sense of identity by focusing on specific events and people that are deemed the most significant for a nation or a group with common interests. Generally, a historian's work is denoted by an effort to tell a form of the truth, though it is seldom the case that any writing is actually objective. In the Middle Ages, in particular, as scholars recognize and debate, there is often a blurring of the boundaries between truth and fiction, between factual prose and the imaginative reconstruction of events.

We can go back to the Anglo-Saxon period momentarily to see this exemplified in the earliest manuscript of *The Anglo-Saxon Chronicle*. This work was begun in the late 9th century, and, through a number of manuscript witnesses, it tells the history of England from biblical times to the middle of the 12th century. It had a diverse audience of religious and lay people and its influence was wide-ranging, as we shall see. The *Chronicle* gives a year-by-year account of important events, though some years are blank, and most focus is on male religious figures, kings, and noblemen. Poems are occasionally embedded within the *Chronicle*, forming an integral part of the usually factual framework.

Among these is *The Battle of Brunanburh*, an alliterative poem which tells the story of King Athelstan's glorious victory over the Vikings, the men of the north, and the Scots in 937. Revelling in the bloodshed of the battlefield, the poet makes out of Athelstan's victory an event of national and historical significance resounding throughout the island. He directly links the glorious Athelstan with his Anglo-Saxon settler-ancestors who destroyed the (sinful, and thus divinely punished) Welsh and took control of large parts of the island:

> Never was there a greater slaughter
> of people killed on this island
> by the sword's edge, even up until now
> or before this, of which the books of ancient scholars
> tell us; that is since from the east
> the Angles and Saxons arrived up
> over the broad seas to seek Britain,
> proud warriors, they overcame the Welsh,
> noble warriors, eager for glory, they conquered the country.

Set within the context of the *Chronicle's* prose annals, *The Battle of Brunanburh* is framed by the achievements of Athelstan's reign in its entirety (924–40). This poem has distinctive nationalistic overtones, seeking to unite and to promote a sense of the shared triumphant destiny of the English in the 10th century. It certainly shows these 10th-century Anglo-Saxons were keenly aware of their historical past. Within the *Chronicle*, though, this past is intermingled with fiction, too, creating for these early medieval kings of England an ancestry that went back to the Bible, but via the mythical Woden, the mythical Beaw, Noah, and Adam.

Such ancient origins for the English kings not only validated their right to the throne, but also sacralized it: they ruled with a traceable inheritance of more than thirty generations to the original divinely created man. Obviously preposterous, such originary myths nevertheless bolstered the monarchy in turbulent times, and helped to consolidate the dynasty. Other originary myths encouraging a cohesive national or tribal identity and enhancing pride in the achievements and prowess of ancestors are produced throughout medieval Europe. Such stories were passed on orally for hundreds of years—memorized and retold: embellished, expanded, and eventually written down for posterity.

The Irish *Táin Bó Cúailnge* (*The Cattle Raid of Cooley*), one version of which is written down in the 12th century *Lebor Laignech* (*Book of Leinster*), refers to very early Celtic society, via these multiple retellings over the centuries. It relates the story of an attempt by Queen Medb to acquire the famous Brown Bull of Cooley, so she can equal the possessions of her husband, King Ailill. There follows a complex sequence of events that pitch warriors of Medb's kingdom of Connacht against other warriors from throughout Ireland. The bull is eventually acquired for Medb, but in the process some of the most heroic fighters from all sides are killed, including the Ulsterman Cú Chulainn—the greatest hero of them all, descended from a god. This heroic tale, like others from Irish and shared Scottish literature, and like stories from early England and Wales in the period, focuses a great deal on the customs and ways of life of a society that is far earlier than the date of the work's survival in writing, suggesting how important to the Irish the transmission of this early culture was for their own sense of themselves and their history.

## Identifying with literary heroes

As the Middle Ages progressed, these national narratives develop into fuller histories from the 12th century onwards. This later period also sees the evolution of chivalric and historical romance, when heroes are knights who undertake tasks for the sake of love and pursue spiritual and personal growth through individual achievement. In the simplest terms, this is in contrast to the more social and communal ethos of the warrior in earlier heroic poetry and prose. Where, for example, Beowulf fights to save his entire nation from a fire-breathing dragon, in the late 14th-century courtly romance by Chaucer, *The Knight's Tale*, the two knightly protagonists fight for the hand of the beautiful

Emelye. *The Knight's Tale* is set in Athens in classical times (a 'Matter of Rome' romance) and is based on the *Teseida*, written by the Italian poet Boccaccio in *c.*1341. Chaucer's lengthy narrative begins with the claim that the *Tale* is composed 'as olde stories tellen us' ('as old histories tell us'), providing authenticity for his story and lending an air of truth to his fiction.

In a similar manner, medieval historians themselves recounted the deeds of kings and bishops in full narratives, fleshing out sparse factual detail with imagined dialogue, and stories of relevant legends and myths. Henry of Huntingdon's *Historia Anglorum* (*History of England*), which ends with events in 1154, drew upon all manner of sources in its composition, including ecclesiastical documents, poetry, other chronicles, and saints' lives. This amalgamation of different kinds of source materials of originally varying perspective and intended function illustrates something very interesting about medieval literature; namely, the permeability of genres and the flexibility of composition.

The 12th century thus saw the burgeoning of the romance, a major genre with multiple sub-genres, which quickly established itself as a favourite of the aristocracy, especially from the reign of Henry II and his wife Eleanor of Aquitaine. The courtly romance—with its attention to love, fellowship, loyalty, generosity, and piety of the chivalric knightly code—was cultivated by the French royalty and noble families in Britain and Ireland in the High Middle Ages, and provided a certain audience for narratives of knightly deeds and tales of pure love. Romance often used historical or pseudo-historical figures from real and imagined past cultures to demonstrate then-contemporary ideals, providing moral instruction through positive example and assisting in creating a sense of shared identity and shared values among the audience.

Romance protagonists demonstrated the aspirations of actual courtly life; and some of the greatest heroes in medieval literature emerge at this time, such as Lancelot, Gawain, Horn, and Guy of Warwick, and, the most inspiring of all heroes—King Arthur (all 'Matter of Britain' romance protagaonists). From the middle of the 12th century onwards, this appropriation of British historical figures into French, Latin, and English poetry and prose is part of a larger pattern of the recasting of history, legend, and myth into new narrative forms. These texts were read and understood in a broader cultural context of multilingualism, settlement, and regional or national interests. Surviving texts from legislation to charters and histories at this time suggest efforts to codify and structure new societies that were emerging as a result of conquest, most dramatically exemplified by the Normans' Conquest of England in 1066, and their subsequent efforts to colonize the Irish and the Welsh. From the later 12th to the early 16th centuries, British and Irish societies embraced multilingualism, innovative forms of literary expression, new administrative processes, the foundation of chartered towns, the rise of the merchant classes, the institutionalization of the church and its methods of pastoral care, new religious orders, and the gradual development of complex literacies. Such was the transformation of later medieval culture.

In Wales, writing in Welsh in the 12th and 13th centuries was diverse, but much of it effectively created a sense of national identity, even while other languages were in use in Wales—from the Latin of churchmen and women, to the French of the nobility, and the English of many, particularly along the Marches. Rather like the emergence in 12th-century Ireland of some of the major manuscripts containing Irish texts, so too, in the same period of colonization by the Normans, Welsh works of literature, old and new, emulative and innovative, emerged in writing.

It is to the post-Conquest period (1066–1200) that the Four Branches of the *Mabinogi* can be dated, as well as the *Brut y Tywysogion* (*Chronicle of the Princes*); and some of the greatest poetry in medieval Welsh. A family of court poets that flourished at this time were Meilyr Brydydd ap Mabon (1081–1137), his son Gwalchmai ap Meilyr, and *his* sons Meilyr ap Gwalchmai and Einion. All were the poets of princes, rewarded by their aristocratic patrons for the work that they created. In this, they are part of a larger group of poets known as *Y Gogynfeirdd*. Their concerns are praise of those whose courts they inhabit, concern for their own souls, appreciation of their country and the traditions in which they work, and the deliberate nurturing of a collective identity distinctively Welsh.

## Hybrid cultures

An author whose work illustrates the difficulties of using terms like 'national' or even 'regional identity' in this period is the Welsh-Norman eminent churchman and scholar Gerald of Wales, or Giraldus Cambrensis (1146–1223). His two most famous Latin works are journeys through Wales and Ireland. In 1185, he accompanied Prince John (later King John) on an expedition to Ireland, which he then described in his *Topographia Hibernica* (*Topography of Ireland*). The *Itinerarium Cambriae* (*Itinerary through Wales*), which he wrote in 1191, detailed his journey with Baldwin, Archbishop of Canterbury, when they attempted to drum up support for the Third Crusade.

In these works, the dynamics of a mixed heritage, a climate of conquest, and the views of an erudite man about those less learned come to the fore. These are tempered by a keen wit and keen eye, and, in the case of writing on his own Welsh land and people, Gerald clearly does identify with some of what he sees some of the time. But he is also discerning in his literate sensibilities, sufficient to give us an insight into contemporary poetry and national literate cultures with their own modes of composing. It is perhaps at this time that the expression of difference begins to be analysed and confidently stated. Indeed, so significant are Gerald's observations, since he makes important distinctions as well as comparisons, that it is worth giving the full flavour of what he has to say in the *Itinerary* Book I, Chapter xii:

> In their narrative poems and their formal speeches [the Welsh] are so inventive and ingenious that they produce works of art when using their native tongue that are at once wonderful and very original, both in the words and the sentiments expressed. Thus one will find many poets in Wales, whom they call bards... They delight in alliteration in preference to any other rhetorical device, and especially the kind which links together the first letters or syllables of words... Here are two examples in Welsh:
>
> Dychaun Dyu da dy unic.
> *God will provide comfort for the lonely man.*
> Erbyn dibuilh puilh paraut.
> *Guard yourself against evil desire.*
> Here are three in English:
> God is togedere gamen and wisdom.
> *Entertainment and wisdom are good together.*
> Ne hat nocht al sor isaid, ne al sorghe atwite.
> *There is nothing to be had by uttering every sorrow, or blaming others for misfortune.*
> Betere is red thene rap, and liste thene lither streignthe.
> *Being prepared is better than haste and caution than misplaced strength.*
>
> ...This device of alliteration does not occur in any other language that I know of as much as it is in English and Welsh. It is surprising, indeed, that French, which is so well adorned in other respects, should never make full use of this particular one, whereas other languages have so entirely adopted it. I cannot believe that the Welsh and the English, so different and antagonistic to each other, could ever have consciously agreed in the use of this rhetorical figure.

Gerald's provision of this information in his *Itinerary* is useful and important in a number of ways. He demonstrates, first of all, his own high level of learning and literary understanding. Despite writing in Latin throughout all of his oeuvre, here, and elsewhere, he acknowledges the existence and value of the various major written vernaculars in play in his own lifetime: French, Welsh, English, and indeed, he talks about northern England, where the language was influenced by Danish and Norwegian. More than this, though, he makes explicit literary difference, as exemplified through language and style, a difference that can be drawn along national and regional lines. Part of what makes identity important here, then, is that we learn more about who we are by understanding who we are not.

Gerald explicitly wants his audience to see and understand the ways in which poetic traditions and rhetoric can be allied to national literary forms that, for the English and Welsh who are normally at odds, function through shared alliterative patterning. The English poetic style that he chooses to demonstrate is not the English that would dominate in the 13th century—verse that rhymed, influenced by the French tradition; but, rather, the English of the Anglo-Saxon tradition. And these are verse-lines, some extracted from larger works, that might most pertinently be thought of as somewhat proverbial, idiomatic, with a gnomic function; that is, they are embedded in popular literary culture, well-known universal truths—common sense, as we might think of it.

## Regional identity through dialect

Literary identities forged through language, but also style of composition, retained great significance throughout the later medieval period, particularly because Britain and Ireland were not just multilingual, but, within that, multidialectal, too. In England after the 12th century, the native Old English language began to change dramatically, partly because of the influx of French, Latin, and, to a lesser extent, Scandinavian loanwords; and partly because scribal training in a standardized English writing no longer happened. Spelling, word choice, and grammar, rather than being a kind of authorized version like late West Saxon, became instead more dependent on the personal choices of author and scribe, heavily influenced by the forms particular to regions of a writer or scribe's origin. At the same time, regular French language use increased during the 13th and 14th centuries to include not just the aristocracy and educated elite, but also the emergent bourgeoisie and merchant classes (see Box 6).

### Box 6  Middle English literature

Middle English flourished in the 14th and 15th centuries, but notable texts were composed as early as c.1170, when the penitential verse, *Poema morale*, was written. By 1200, the standard literary language (late West Saxon) had broken down, and English texts from the 13th to the 15th centuries are written in the dialect of their authors and scribes, so spelling and vocabulary tend to vary considerably.

From 1170, verse had multiple metrical forms, including rhyme, often influenced by French. Many notable poetic and prose works survive from this highly dynamic multilingual and multicultural time in English literary production, and authors such as Geoffrey Chaucer, William Langland, and Thomas Malory are especially important. As was typical of the period, authors built on the works of earlier authorities; Layamon's early 13th-century chronicle, *Brut*, adapted the work of earlier writers in Latin (Geoffrey of Monmouth) and French (Wace) to tell the poetic history of Britain, founded by Brutus of Troy. As literacy increased, personal compendia of poetry and prose illustrate the extension of manuscript production from the ecclesiastical institution into the nobility's households. Large numbers of religious tracts, books of sermons, histories, and romances are among the many texts created during this rich period of literary production.

Added to this linguistic fluidity was the preference in specific regions for particular forms of poetry; that is, regionalization of literature became an important and notable feature of English in the later part of the Middle Ages. So, for example, poetry known as tail-rhyme verse was popular in the East Anglian region of England in the 14th and 15th centuries. The opening of the 15th-century poem *Athelston*, which is a romance set in a fictionalized world of the Anglo-Saxons, shows this kind of tail-rhyme where the rhyme scheme is aabccb:

> Lord, þat is off myʒtys most,
> *Lord, that is of mightiness most,*
> Fadyr and sone and holy gost,
> *Father and son and holy ghost.*
> Bryng us out off synne.
> *Bring us out of sin.*
> And lene us grace so forto wyrke
> *And grant us grace so that we work*
> To love boþe God and holy kyrke,
> *To love both God and holy church,*
> Þat we may hevene wynne.
> *That we may heaven win.*

In contrast to this rhyme scheme in the east, non-rhyming alliterative verse dominated in the west and north of England, in an arguably unbroken tradition from the Anglo-Saxon period. Other, newer forms of poetry were also developed in parallel, like the octosyllabic rhyming couplets (eight syllable lines paired through rhyme) of the Nun of Barking's French *La Vie d'Édouard le confesseur*, or the later Rhyme Royal of Chaucer's major romance, *Troilus and Criseyde*.

So it is that by the later 14th century, what had once been a fairly consistent style and dialect of English literary production had become diverse in terms of sound, spelling, vocabulary, and poetic style. When English became firmly re-established as a major chosen literary medium (having been subordinated to French and Latin) around the reign of Richard II (d. 1399), what appeared could be identified by dialect. Thus, the three greatest English poetic works of the High Middle Ages—Chaucer's *Canterbury Tales*, *Sir Gawain and the Green Knight*, and *Piers Plowman*—while roughly contemporary, are yet very different to look at and to read.

A number of versions of the long religious and didactic poem known as *Piers Plowman* exist, written over many years of effort by a certain William Langland in the 1360s to, perhaps, the late 1380s. The poem concerns the search for Truth (God) by the protagonist and dreamer, Will, who represents Everyman. He has an innovative sequence of dream visions in which he encounters real and allegorical characters on his journey, including the king and his court, Conscience, Reason, and a ploughman named Piers. The poem itself is set in the west of England, and is written in alliterative verse, with two half-lines linked by stressed syllables which begin with the same sound: <s> in line 1 below, <sh> in line 2, <h> in line 3, and so on. The effect of this is that, in great lines of poetry (and *Piers Plowman* is great poetry), the sound of the alliterating syllables generally supports and helps to emphasize and reinforce the meaning. In this spring opening then, a *reverdie* in literary terms, the softly articulated consonants help set a peaceful, contemplative scene, only broken in line 6 by the more abrasive repetition of <f>.

> In a somer seson, whan softe was the sonne,
> *In a summer season, when the sun was soft,*
> I shoop me into shroudes as I a sheep were,
> *I dressed myself as if I were a shepherd*
> In habite as an heremite unholy of werkes;
> *In the outfit of a hermit, unholy in deeds;*
> Wente wide in this world wondres to here.
> *I went widely through this world to hear marvels.*

> Ac on a May morwenynge on Malverne hilles
> *But on a May morning in the Malvern Hilles*
> Me bifel a ferly, of fairye me thoghte.
> *I had a vision; it seemed to be otherworldly.*

In another contemporary text by an anonymous author, alliterative verse is also used. This text is the 2,530-line, four-part Arthurian romance, *Sir Gawain and the Green Knight*, which survives uniquely in London, British Library, Cotton Nero A. x. It was probably written for the household of a noble person somewhere in the northwest of England towards the end of the 14th century, and it is one of the most compelling and action-packed poems of any period. The form of this poem, while alliterative, is designed around a stanza, which ends with a short bob and a four-line wheel; the bob generally contains matter of great significance. What is also notable about *Sir Gawain* and the three poems in the same manuscript (*Patience*, *Cleanness*, and *Pearl*) is how different its dialect is from *Piers Plowman* or from Chaucer's English; this is partly due to a much higher percentage of the vocabulary in *Sir Gawain* being of Scandinavian, or Old Norse, origin. This makes it, on an initial reading, quite difficult to access now, since a great deal of the vocabulary has died out. Lines 134–40 in Fitt (Part) 1 begin with the quietening down of Arthur's court at Camelot as the New Year celebratory feast is served. As the knights and their ladies eat their meal, there is a sudden interruption:

> For uneþe watz þe noyce not a whyle sesed,
> *For hardly had the noise been ceased a moment,*
> And þe fyrst cource in þe court kyndely served,
> *And the first course of the meal in the court politely served,*
> Þer hales in at þe halle dor an aghlich mayster,
> *When there rushes in at the hall door a fearsome lord,*
> On þe most on þe molde on mesure hyghe;
> *One of the biggest on the earth in measure of height;*

Fro þe swyre to þe swange so sware and so þik,

*From the neck to the middle so sturdy and thick-set*

And his lyndes and his lymes so longe and so grete,

*And his loins and his limbs so long and so great*

Half-etayn in erde I hope þat he were.

*That half-giant on earth I believed that he could be.*

Not only is this half-giant terrifyingly huge, fearsome, and impolite in breaking into the feast, but, as the poem's audience quickly learns, he is also green from head to toe and he is riding a green horse. The poem's focus on identity is more than literary here: who belongs to the world of the human and who does not? How does a community deal with antagonistic interlopers? What happens when the ethics and the *mores* of an entire system like the chivalric code with its courtly ideals cannot be maintained? This poem, like many others in the languages of later medieval Britain and Ireland, seeks through entertainment and instruction to address these key social and cultural questions.

# Chapter 4
# Individual and community

## Collective ideals

In *Sir Gawain and the Green Knight* and *Piers Plowman*,
contemporary late 14th-century poems that are widely studied still,
the poets examine how the individual represents and espouses the
values of their society. *Sir Gawain* is a great Arthurian romance
derived, in part, from Celtic and French literary tradition and
English originary myth claiming the foundation of Britain through
Brutus, whose ancestor was Aeneas. Gawain represents the court
of King Arthur in his arduous solo quest to find the Green Knight.
His shield, painted with a pentangle and an image of the Virgin
Mary, reminds Gawain and the poem's audience of the significance
of the chivalric values of 'fraunchyse', 'felawschyp', 'cortaysye', 'pité',
and 'clannes' ('generosity', 'fellowship', 'courtesy', 'piety', and
'cleanness' or 'purity'), and of a life lived while adhering resolutely
to Christian virtues.

As the representative of the court of Arthur, it is Gawain's duty to
uphold the whole community's value-system, and to reinforce it
through his actions. Among the many foci of the poem is the issue
of whether or not Gawain maintains his integrity, or, at least,
whether his desire to save his own life by concealing a truth is
sufficient to undo him as the epitome of the chivalric code. The
poem demands the engagement and judicious response of an

informed audience familiar with the courtly *mores* under scrutiny; a demand that is also required of a 21st-century audience.

What *Sir Gawain and the Green Knight* illustrates, too, is the poet's interest in the single, thinking man. Gawain's actions are certainly knightly; he defends King Arthur's honour when he comes forward in court to meet the challenge of an exchange of axe-blows offered by the Green Knight (the Beheading Game). He decapitates the Green Knight, who promptly (and both alarmingly and hilariously) picks up his head and rides out of court, reminding Gawain to find and meet him a year hence. Gawain sets out courageously on his quest for the Green Knight from whom he must receive an axe-stroke in return. But Gawain's actions are not necessarily unflinchingly heroic as the story unfolds. He stays at a castle, hosted by a knight, Bertilak (whose magical alter ego is the Green Knight), and we are shown something of Gawain's fallibility when he seeks to protect his life by keeping a girdle with supposed magical powers given to him by the wife of his host. As the Green Knight gets ready to bring down the axe on the neck of the kneeling Gawain, the poet reveals the absolute humanness of the knight:

> Bot Gawayn on þat giserne glyfte hym bysyde
> *But Gawain on that battle-axe glanced sideways*
> As hit com glydande adoun on glode hym to schende,
> *As it came gliding down in a flash to destroy him,*
> And schranke a lytel with þe schulderes for þe scharp yrne.
> *And shrank a little with his shoulders from the sharp steel.*

The swiftness of this sequence (emphasized and supported by the alliterating syllables) reveals a knight in fear for his life, an insight into an individual response that is entirely understandable. Easy to empathize with, too, perhaps, is Gawain's shame when he is caught out and called a coward by the Green Knight, who knows that his wife gave Gawain the girdle. But this individual shame that Gawain feels is dismissed by Arthur's court when

Gawain returns and tells his story, showing them the girdle—his 'token of untrawþe' ('token of infidelity') that he now wears permanently. His fellow courtiers see instead his courage and true virtue in taking on and surviving the challenge of the Green Knight and take it as an honour to the court and the ethos of the Round Table. They thus adopt the girdle as a token of their collective support for Gawain, recognizing in the valiant actions of the individual the renown of the community.

Many other medieval romances highlight the actions of individual knights working on behalf of their community through the solo quest. Anglo-Norman families in the later 12th and 13th centuries seemed particularly keen on stories that spoke to them of England as they sought to establish their new English heritage. The community depicted in some of these romances (like *Lai d'Haveloc* or *Havelock the Dane* and *Boeve* or *Bevis of Hampton*) could be an entire kingdom. This is the case in the 13th-century Middle English poem *King Horn*, adapted from a now-lost French poem, which must itself have been related to one of the best surviving insular French poems, the *Roman de Horn* (*Romance of Horn*), written around 1170 by a certain Thomas.

Horn, as a king in search of vengeance for the death of his father and loss of his kingdom, travels overseas with his group of dedicated followers, a small band of trusted warriors who are similar to the Germanic Heroic *comitatus* (lord's troop of warriors) from the earlier medieval period. He helps another king in battles against enemies, and falls in love with the king's daughter. To prove himself, Horn alone undertakes his exploits and hand-to-hand combat against treacherous opponents and giant antagonists, and after journeying from place to place, and rescuing his beloved from an enforced marriage, he regains his country, dividing all the spoils among his most faithful comrades. The poem represents an effective commingling of the epic—with its grand scale and geography of the text—and the romantic, with the love interest, and the themes of exile and return, loyalty and betrayal.

Horn is always instantly recognizable to those he encounters as a noble and heroic character, because he is beautiful; and the action of this poem is rapidly told, particularly in the English version where there is sparse detail and little character delineation. This early romance essentially demonstrates the ideal hero's resilient engagement with villainous enemies (such as the gigantic Saracens, typical villains in the French poetic 'songs of deeds', the *chansons de geste*). In these narratives with the happy ending necessary in romance, virtue eventually defeats vice; nobility of character and courageous action is victorious over evil. Evil takes the form of the non-Christian in these romances, such that the aspirations of a religiously inspired Christian community are embodied in the pious efforts of the knight.

The 12th century, then, sees a very important literary-cultural shift from the Germanic Heroic demonstrations of lordly treasure-giving, absolute loyalty between lord and *comitatus*, and public declarations and acts of bravery, to the more privately motivated individual quests of knights, who fight for their king, certainly, but also for the love of a lady. The audience were entertained and educated through these poems; their aspirations and desires are reflected in them, too. These romances' emphases on the knightly, the chivalric, and love are inspired predominantly by French literature—the songs and stories of the itinerant troubadour (southern French) or trouvère (northern) as they were adapted into longer narrative form.

One of the most famous continental romance writers was Chrétien de Troyes, a French trouvère, who was associated with the court of Marie de Champagne, the daughter of Eleanor of Aquitaine. Chrétien built on the fundamentally important Arthurian legend established earlier in the 12th century by Geoffrey of Monmouth. This was the first work to establish the legend of Arthur and to create the myth of the foundation of Britain by Brutus, descendant of Aeneas. Geoffrey of Monmouth's work was adapted into French by the Plantagenet court poet Wace in the 1150s. It was Wace who introduced the Round Table into the narrative.

Geoffrey of Monmouth and Wace, among others, initiated the immensely significant literary tradition of the Arthurian tale that was taken up by Chrétien around the 1170s, when his highly influential cycle included *Yvain*, *Perceval*, *Lancelot*, and *Eric and Enide*. These Arthurian romances appeared to have particular purchase in royal courtly circles in France and England at first, but the genre of romance more generally became highly popular in the context of noble families. These families included regional baronial households, the homes of nobles, and, increasingly, the homes of wealthy professionals within the context of rapidly developing urbanization. Any one or more of these audiences might have been happy to receive the early 13th-century version of Arthur's story written in English by Layamon, and included in his adventure-packed alliterative poem, the *Brut*.

## On proper conduct

Some of the Welsh prose texts regarded as part of the collection known as the *Mabinogi* (or *Mabinogion*, as their 19th-century editor, Charlotte Guest, called them) share at least a common source with Chretien de Troyes's work. In the Welsh tradition, the *Three Romances* (*Y Tair Rhamant*)—*Owain*, *Peredur*, and *Geraint and Enid*—are a subset of the group of eleven stories that nowadays form the *Mabinogi*, datable to the later 11th and 12th centuries. Single stories exist in six different manuscripts or fragments of manuscripts, the earliest of which is from the second half of the 13th century; that is, much later than the probable dates of the prose works' original, oral compositions. These anonymous narratives have different authors, and they relate legends about Welsh kings and princes and their families, who must deal with various opponents and troubles, some involving magic and the otherworld.

The lively and sometimes complicated plots instruct the audience in patience, perseverance, and self-reliance. Some of them, such as the Four Branches, focus on a variety of protagonists from Wales, England, and Ireland, with legendary and mythical elements that are ancient, told and retold by the keepers of stories, the *cyfarwyddyd*. One character—Pryderi—appears in all Four Branches. In the first branch, he is the son born to Pwyll, lord of Dyfed, and Rhiannon, the 'Great Queen'. Pryderi disappears on the night of his birth, and is found and brought up by others, only to be restored in adulthood to his parents, his mother having been accused of murder at his disappearance. In the second branch, he is one of the warriors who survives conflict between the British and the Irish kings, Bran and Matholwch. In the third, Pryderi and his mother fight a sequence of enchantments, overcoming all manner of obstacles; and in the fourth branch, Pryderi dies in a war between Welsh kingdoms. He seems to have been, perhaps like Arthur himself, an early Welsh hero, who makes appearances in texts other than the *Mabinogi*, such as the *Book of Taliesin*, and the *Spoils of Annwn*.

The catalogue poem *Englynion y Beddau* (*Verses of the Graves*) lists where Wales's great heroes are buried and one of them is Pryderi. It is contained in the mid-13th-century *Llyfr Du Caerfyrddin* (*Black Book of Carmarthen*, digitized in full as Aberystwyth, National Library of Wales, Peniarth 1). Arthur also appears among this group of Welsh warrior elite, along with Pryderi, King of Dyfed, and Gwallwg, an early Welsh warrior, nephew of Caradwc:

> En Aber Gwenoli y mae bet Pryderi
> *At Aber Gwenoli is the grave of Pryderi*
> yny terev tonnev tir:
> *where the waves beat against the land;*
> yg Karrauc bet Gwallauc Hir.
> *at Carrawg is the grave of Gwallawg Hir.*

Perhaps this list of the 'graves of the great' functions more poignantly than a lengthy romance narrative? The grave ties the legendary hero to the land and makes the legend real: an embodiment of ancient steadfastness and courage that can be visited and marked. The *Verses of the Graves*, with its long list of short *englynion*, operates as a kind of incantation to call up collective memories; a piling up of the splendour of the dead who rest, remembered, among the living. The single scribe of Peniarth 1, who may have been an Augustinian canon at Carmarthen in south Wales, seems to have worked on this manuscript for years, himself piling up texts that served to please and instruct and tell histories. As a canon writing such an overwhelmingly legible manuscript it might have been his intention to read the anthology aloud to edify a local Welsh-speaking population and to inspire them communally with the knowledge of heroes, at a time when those people were most in need of a sense of their country's historical glories.

## Building a communion

Canons, monks, and secular clergy in the medieval period were duty-bound by their Christian mission to create social stability and unity through the preaching of God's word. Gospels, sermons, saints' lives, and other religious books, like Confessionals and Penitentials, exist in abundance. In the Anglo-Saxon period, Old English sermons form the largest generic corpus of vernacular material that survives. Similarly, saints' lives were written, translated, and copied throughout the period. Far from being a dull read, saints' lives can be closely allied with romance, because both genres share particular features in common, including the hero (or heroine) who resists all forms of torment in a quest to stay resolutely on God's side. Indeed, in a very popular romance like *Gui de Warewic* (*Guy of Warwick*), or others like *Octavian* or *The King of Tars*, significant elements of the saint's life (or the hagiographic) inform aspects of the plot and characterization, including the Christian hero's long-suffering, his pious spirituality, and his devotional acts alongside his valiant deeds. The wide dissemination of these romances suggests a broad audience for the saintly hero.

Whereas a great many medieval poems tend to be anonymously composed, with sermons and saints' lives a good number of authors are known, including Rhygyfarch ap Sulien, a Welsh cleric at Llanbadarn Fawr in the later 11th century, who wrote a Latin *Life of St David*; William of Malmesbury, the prodigious 12th-century monk and historiographer, who translated an English *Life of St Wulfstan* into Latin (among many other works); and Clemence of Barking, a female hagiographer, who wrote the octosyllabic verse *Vie de Sainte Catherine*, a French life of St Catherine of Alexandria, in the late 12th century. The hagiographic genre had very great appeal in all the languages of the Middle Ages. In English, Ælfric, Abbot of Eynsham (d. 1010), wrote a sequence of saints' lives in a form of vernacular alliterative prose for the entire church year; and a cycle of saints' lives, the *Golden Legend*, composed in Latin by the Italian Jacobus de Voragine, became one of the most important works of devotion throughout later medieval Europe.

In the 15th century, the poet and friar Osbern Bokenham (d. *c.*1464) wrote the *Legendys of Hooly Wummen*. It narrates thirteen narratives of female saints, some of which are written for specific patrons in the East Anglian area in which Bokenham lived and worked. These individual saints' lives, written to inspire devotion, include the most beloved holy women: Margaret, Katherine, Agnes, Lucy, Anne, Dorothy, and Cecilia. A number of these were legendary female virgin martyrs, executed in the period of the Roman persecutions of Christians in the 3rd or early 4th centuries. The lives tend to follow a similar pattern and can seem quite formulaic; thus, the saints are beautiful young Christians desired by older heathen men, who torture the women to try and break their will, only to fail as the women are protected by God.

The persecutors resort to extreme brutality, and usually decapitation of the saint. The saint performs miracles throughout her ordeal and posthumously.

It is fascinating to know that these saints' lives were required reading matter for aristocratic young women and these hagiographies were also regularly read out at the appropriate saint's festival in the church year. A saint like Margaret, who was imprisoned by her torturer, and supposedly swallowed by a dragon sent by the Devil, became the patron saint of women in childbirth, presumably because she burst, unharmed, out of the dragon's stomach when she made the sign of the cross. Quite how medieval women were supposed to live up to the high standards of resolve and fortitude exemplified by these (often fictional) saints is an interesting question; the fact that these lives were loved by readers in this period suggests a desire to witness and participate in stories that illustrated courage and resilience through suffering, and always ended happily (as in romance, indeed) with heavenly repatriation.

There is no doubt that women were significant consumers of female saints' lives. Evidence exists in a variety of forms: in the collections of work specifically for female audiences, such as the English *Katherine-Group* of Lives of Katherine, Margaret, and Juliana. These were associated with female communities of anchoresses (religious women who undertook a life of isolated contemplation of God) in the West Midlands at the beginning of the 13th century. In Chaucer's writings, too, it is clear that women and hagiography were closely associated; in the *Canterbury Tales*, the Second Nun tells a standard hagiography of St Cecilia's suffering and salvation; and in *Troilus and Criseyde*, Criseyde glibly says she should be reading holy saints' lives.

Large collections of saints' lives, like the multi-manuscript cycle the *South English Legendary*, written by multiple authors in the late 13th and 14th centuries, had a major impact, suggesting that knowing about the lives of sanctified individuals contributed considerably to a communal ideal of religious devotion. Local saints' lives were composed, too, promoting institutions and bringing in visitors from all over a region in veneration of the saint; thus, a number of hagiographies and references to Irish saints, such as Brigid, Patrick, and Molaise, occur in the 15th-century Irish *Book of Lismore* (*Leabhar Mhic Cárthaigh Riabhaigh*), for example. These books themselves suggest a devoted community of worshippers, and attempts to build a sense of shared history and common heritage through text.

## From communion to community

The symbiotic relationship between the individual and the community both within a text and as a result of textual remembrance is of great importance, particularly in a period where personal literacy—the ability to pick up a text and read it oneself—was a scarce skill. Public Christian communities took many forms from boisterous church congregations to small groups of attentive devotees.

The *Ancrene Wisse*, or *Ancrene Riwle*, is a *Guide for Anchoresses* associated with the *Katherine Group* of saints' lives, and another text on virginity called *Hali Meiðhad* (*Holy Maidenhood*). The *Ancrene Wisse* was written by a male religious author to assist three aristocratic women in their avowed lives as contemplatives, shut up in a cell-like room attached to a church with a squint to allow them to peer into the church and participate remotely in the community. Such medieval anchor-holds are still to be seen adjacent to churches such as Skipton, in Yorkshire.

The *Ancrene Wisse*, composed *c*.1225, was remarkably popular and survives in English in eleven manuscript versions, as well as in four translations into French and four into Latin, and it was also adapted for male anchorites and for larger groups of religious solitaries. It exemplifies rather well the ways in which the individual functioned as part of a larger community, while, to an extent, being cut off from that community. The author creates the *Guide* to instruct the anchoresses in how they should live both their outer, bodily lives and their inner, spiritual lives. They are advised about what they should wear: 'wel mei don of ower cla∂ beo hit hwit, beo hit blac, bute hit beo unorne' ('it matters not whether your clothes are white or black, except that they are plain'); that they should not have jewellery; and that they can keep no animals, except a cat. The writer advises that they should build their own small textual community by reading to the women serving the needs of the anchoress: 'ʒe ancres ahen þis leaste stucche reden to ower wummen euche wike eanes aþet ha hit cunnen' ('You anchoresses ought to read this last section [on the Outer Rule] to your women once each week until they know it'). In teaching the *Guide*, the adviser points out, the anchoress will be sure to learn it and keep it devoutly herself.

This public display, intended to teach, inspire, and encourage the adherence to a faithful Christian life, also motivates the most communal of literature: drama. Dramatic performances of moments from the Christian story had long been part of the liturgy or church service, but in the later Middle Ages organized dramas became an established part of urban and village life. In particular cases, these were put on by the laity for the laity (often Guildsmen of the town were responsible for specific parts), and centred on the life and events of Christ, or the exemplary Christian.

Two plays survive from medieval Dublin in Ireland: *The Play of the Sacrament*, and the earlier 15th-century English morality play *The Pride of Life*. In England, the York Cycle of mystery plays, which are now performed every four years, emerged in the later 14th century as a sequence of dramatic pageants on wagons performed through the city, on or around the day of the procession on the Corpus Christi feast. These wagons were each sponsored by one of the craft guilds to perform the highlights of the Christian story from the Creation to the Nativity, to the Crucifixion, to the Last Judgement. The wagons would be driven around the town, stopping to perform the pageant at a particular station in sequence lasting all day and into the night.

Other towns—notably Chester, Coventry, and Wakefield—also have surviving dramatic cycle texts, among the most studied being the *Second Shepherd's Play*, written by the Wakefield Master, and contained within the Towneley manuscript along with the other thirty-one relatively brief Wakefield plays. There are moments of absolute comedy in this play, as there are in many others, for comedy compels attention and instructs without seeming to. Yet other cycle plays survive from East Anglian centres, where the dramas were generally performed on open-air stages, rather than wagons. Further plays exist that are less about biblical events and salvation history, and more about morality, where characters represent types, or the whole of humanity, such as Humankind in *The Castle of Perseverance*, a morality play from the early 15th century.

Three mystery plays in a Cornish trilogy, the *Ordinalia*, focus on the Origin of the World, the Passion of Christ, and the Resurrection of the Lord (*Ordinale de origine mundi*, *Passio Domini Nostri Jhesu Christi*, and *Ordinale de Resurrexione Domini*) (see Box 7). These survive in three manuscript versions, the earliest of which is Oxford, Bodleian Library, Bodley 791. Performed over three days, these plays urged an audience to understand the basic episodes in the Christian tradition by showing the events to assembled individuals in a large public space. Through humour and fast-paced dialogue, the plays provide huge entertainment as well as core salvific instruction.

This trilogy was written down in the later 14th century, and while it is composed predominantly in Middle Cornish, there are also bits and pieces of Latin, English, and French. Linking all three parts of the *Ordinalia* is the story of the Holy Rood, the tree upon

Individual and community

which Christ was crucified. Legend has it this tree grew from a seed that came from the Tree of the Knowledge of Good and Evil in the Garden of Eden. The seed was buried with Adam and grew into a tree itself—the same tree that was subsequently brought to the Temple of Solomon, and thereafter used to crucify Christ.

In Cornish, too, is the rare survival of a saint's life written as a drama: that of St Meriasek, a Breton saint. *Beunans Meriasek* is contained in an early 16th-century paper manuscript (Aberystwyth, National Library of Wales, Peniarth 105B (see Figure 4)), and tells the story of the saint's life, miraculous

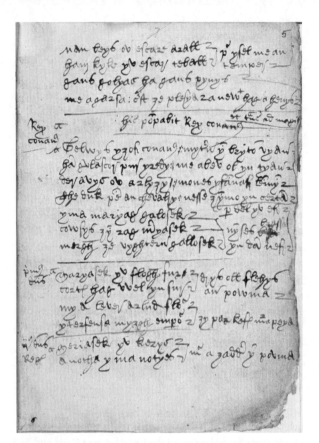

**4.** *Beunans Meriasek*, the Cornish drama *The Life of St Meriasek*, Aberystwyth, National Library of Wales, Peniarth 105B, folio 5r.

abilities, and death, as bishop of Vannes. As is the case with the *Ordinalia*, the framework of the drama—the rubrics and directions for the performers—is cast multilingually, using Latin and English, as well as Cornish, suggesting a mixed community of players were accessing this text.

# Chapter 5
# The mighty and the monstrous

## Order and chaos

In medieval societies, religious and secular literature built communities by encouraging and persuading individuals to behave in certain ways, to absorb particular sets of knowledge, and to emulate similar ideals. There is more to it than this, but prescriptive and proscriptive texts exist in all surviving records from the earliest centuries. Some texts are explicitly proscriptive; sermons and a good deal of religious material could be thought of as exhorting against impious and amoral thoughts, words, and deeds in no uncertain terms; and simply forbidding actions that were thought to encourage waywardness, witchcraft, and the abandonment of societally acceptable norms. Other texts, though, like the dynamic and engaging drama that emerged in the 14th and 15th centuries, could proscribe by demonstrating the consequence of evil personified, or by creating visually and aurally repellent enactments of dreadful deeds. Those who maintained control—the church, the elite, local government—persistently sought to maintain order and deter disruptive, immoral, or anti-social behaviour.

Order comes from the delineation of propriety, the regulation of society, the measuring and marking of territory, and the acknowledgement by the majority of what is acceptable. For early

British and Irish people, this would be reflected in settlements being established and borders being respected and remembered. Christian processions at Rogationtide walked along the boundaries of the local parish (and 'beating the bounds' still happens in some townships like Laugharne in south Wales); legal charters written in Latin often included clauses describing in great detail the landmarks that denoted the perimeter of the land being granted.

Burghs, villages, towns, cities, and countries followed laws, whether familial, tribal, local, regional, or national. What lay on the other side of the boundary of these laws resulted in 'outlaws', those who lived beyond order, beyond the familiar, beyond the known. In places inhabited by outlaws, or areas that were unmapped and uninhabited, there lay the dangers of the unknown and people, or things, or spaces that were out of control. As the centuries have progressed, those unknown regions have become further and further removed as exploration reveals much of the world; but still, deep sea, darkest forest, and outer space itself remain marginal, unquantifiable, and potentially (in films, on television, in fiction) filled with monstrosities and imminent disaster.

For the medieval world, the unknown, and thus the potentially monstrous, was closer to home. Without streetlights, without clearly demarcated and deforested landscape, there was a genuine darkness at night that is often difficult to emulate now. It was so much easier to get lost on journeys when there were no compasses, no signs, and sometimes no clear roads to follow. So, the spaces that were safe were inside walls, fences, houses, societies, whereas wilder, uncultivated landscape threatened. In *Sir Gawain and the Green Knight*, when Gawain makes his way to meet the Green Knight, he leaves the warmth of Camelot and enters a forest only to be challenged by countless monsters and wild creatures.

The shadowy land in between places of civilized order presents wonderful opportunities for authors' imaginations. In the Anglo-Saxon literary tradition, many texts can be singled out for attention, including the earliest English romance, *Apollonius of Tyre* (in Cambridge, Corpus Christi College, 201, datable to about 1050), which problematizes monstrosity by having as its primary antagonist someone who should be the epitome of order and rule: a king, Antiochus. He commits incest with his daughter and then kills successive noblemen to cover his tracks, and by so doing, he provides an excellent foil to the hero of the prose tale—Apollonius.

As with many romances, the plot is complex, driven by motifs of exile and return, loyalty and treachery, love and vengeance. This same classical narrative provided the source for Shakespeare's *Pericles*, but was also treated by John Gower—Chaucer's contemporary and friend—an exceptionally talented author, who wrote in Latin, French, and English. Gower included the story in his major English poem, the *Confessio amantis* (*The Lover's Confession*), a consolatory work comprised of a sequence of verse tales, dated to 1390. In the *Confessio*, Antiochus in Apollonius of Tyre is used to exemplify the dangers of lechery. The audience is told that Antiochus' wife has died and:

> His doghter, which was piereles
> *His daughter, who was without comparison*
> Of beauté, duelte aboute him stille;
> *In beauty, dwelled with him still;*
> Bot whanne a man hath welthe at wille,
> *But when a man has wealth in abundance,*
> The fleissh is frele and falleth ofte.
> *The flesh is frail and fails often.*
> And that this maide, tendre and softe,
> *And so this maiden, tender and soft,*
> Which in hire fadres chambres duelte,
> *Who dwelled in her father's chambers,*
> Withinne a time wiste and felte
> *Soon knew and experienced*
> For likinge and concupiscence,
> *Because of desire and physical lust,*

> Withoute insihte of conscience,
> *Without insight from conscience,*
> The fader so with lustes blente,
> *The father, so blinded with lust,*
> That he caste al his hole entente
> *That he set his entire intent*
> His oghne doghter for to spille.
> *Upon the rape of his own daughter.*

There are multiple levels of horror and monstrosity in Gower's depiction of Antiochus, which, line by line, seems to explain the premeditation of his depravity, building up rationalizing of the awful deed and his ghastly intention ('I'm a king and I can have anything; my flesh is weak; she's so beautiful; I really want her; I can have what I want'). 'Conscience', which should guide him, is absent; intellectual insight and spiritual sight are lacking, so that he is simply, but horribly, driven by bodily urges to rape his *own* daughter.

The repulsive actions of Antiochus and his inability to curb his overwhelming physical desires highlight one of the key aspects of monstrosity for medieval writers. In sermons throughout the centuries, preachers railed against permitting the seven (sometimes eight) deadly sins to take hold. Wrath, Lechery, Gluttony, Envy, Avarice, Sloth, and Pride feature in countless tracts, didactic poems, plays, and saints' lives. In many depictions and lists, Pride heads the sins; in others, it is Gluttony. Indeed, a list put together by the early theologian Isidore of Seville outlines whole nations' associations with particular sins: *Ira brittorum, stultitia saxonum, libido scottorum, crudelitas pictorum* ('the anger of the Britons; the foolishness of the Saxons; the lust of the Scots [the *Scotti* are the Irish]; the inhumanity of the Picts').

Asserting the monstrosity of whole races was (and is) one way in which colonizers, or proponents of particular dominant religious beliefs, seek to oppress or control others. William of Malmesbury, probably the finest 12th-century historiographer, in his explication of the Norman divine right to rule through conquest, reviles the English for their drunkenness with its attendant witlessness and loss of national status. In his great Latin *Deeds of the Kings of the English*, the *Gesta regum Anglorum*, which he finished in 1125, he writes in Book 1 that for the English: 'Drinking communally was done by all, and in this habit they made no distinction between night and day ... There followed the vices that accompany drunkenness ... eating food that encouraged intoxication and drinking until they caused themselves to throw up.' For Malmesbury, it was the Normans' ability to control themselves that distinguished them from the conquered, sinful English, though he laments, too, the loss of the Anglo-Saxon realm to the Normans.

## Size matters

Excess and lack of control, lack of *order* in one's own demeanour, created a major form of monstrosity from within society, roundly condemned by authorities, particularly those in the church and particularly those who sought to regulate. In medieval romance, the monstrous outsider was often depicted as a 'Saracen', a universalized type of opponent, instigated by the Christian Crusades against the Muslims for control of the Holy Land in the eastern Mediterranean. These campaigns, beginning in 1096 and lasting all the way into the 15th century, became a major subject of European romance literature, many narratives featuring knightly battles against monstrous Saracens. Through these depictions of ideal knightly heroism, white European crusaders were given models for ostensible right behaviour, and spiritual encouragement for their religious wars.

The oldest surviving version of a *chanson de geste* ('song of heroic deeds') is the 12th-century French *La Chanson de Roland*, *The*

*Song of Roland* (Oxford, Bodleian Library, Digby 23). In this poem, after Charlemagne's army has been engaged in battle against the Saracen in Spain, Roland, the hero of the story, is ambushed by Saracens, and boldly fights to his death, but not before he has blown his ivory horn (the *Olifant*) to summon Charlemagne to take revenge. While many of the Saracen enemy are depicted as worthy opponents—noble and beautiful, though damned—others, like Falsaron in *laisse* 94, brother to the Muslim king, Marsilla, are gigantic, monstrous:

> Suz cel nen at plus encrisme felun;
> *There is no more hardened felon on earth;*
> Entre les dous oilz mult out large le front,
> *Between his two eyes was a very large space,*
> Grant demi pied mesurer i pout hom.
> *It measures at least a half-foot.*

While Falsaron's heathenness is a focus for the poet, the evidence provided for his being a 'hardened felon' is his size, emphasized by the single lingering detail (synecdoche) of the enormous gap between his eyes. The implication is that if the gap between his eyes is six inches, then how big is the rest of him? He looms vast and monstrous into the text.

Later medieval romances in English, French, Welsh, and their multiple reflexes, continue the theme of the Saracen enemy who is overcome by the Christian hero. In texts such as the *Romance of Horn*, *Guy of Warwick*, *Richard Coeur de Lion*, *Otuel*, *The Sultan of Babylon*, and *Beues of Hampton*, the gigantic Saracen is a type, delineated by his monstrous appearance or his skin colour, manifesting, in these good versus evil formulae, inner debility and sinfulness. The Christian protagonist is usually able to demonstrate his overwhelming superiority in a display of combat and virtuous speech that is lauded by the poet. In this way, literary texts contributed to a systematic derogation of the exoticized enemy, bolstering the social and cultural ideals and efforts promoted by European kings, aristocracy, prelates, and popes for centuries. The formulaic nature of this scene though could also, effectively, be appropriated symbolically for the denigration and attempted conquest of any enemy.

Earlier texts explored the nature of monstrosity with startling effect, too, and none more so than the epic Anglo-Saxon poem *Beowulf*. In this poem, the eponymous hero, and greatest of all warriors, Beowulf, arrives at Heorot, the hall of the Danish king, Hroðgar. He comes to help Hroðgar defeat the monster, Grendel, who has attacked and killed Danish warriors for the previous twelve years. Grendel is a complex monster, not least because he is eternally damned through a direct relationship with Cain, the first murderer in the Bible. We are told that Grendel 'carried God's wrath' (*'Godes yrre bær'*) suggesting, ambiguously, that Grendel is the carrier of God's wrath against the very people he attacks, and/or that God is angry with Grendel. He is also depicted as an outsider, haunting the moors, excluded from the joys of the warriors' hall. This may not have elicited a great deal of sympathy from Anglo-Saxon audiences sitting in a hall listening to the poem being recited, conscious of the absolute darkness just beyond the door. It does, though, problematize the nature of evil, the depiction of the monstrous. From a modern perspective, especially, some contemporary readers wonder whether, if monstrosity is innate and inherited, the monster is to blame for its actions? If the monster is permanently outcast, why would it not seek some kind of revenge?

The *Beowulf*-poet creates in Grendel one of the all-time most spectacular monsters. He is a monster about whom we know very specific details, released gradually in the course of the long poem. We learn that he has the name Grendel (who named him?); that he is a fiend from hell ('feond on helle'); that he is man-shaped; that he attacks at night; we know he is an 'āglæca' ('a monster', or, confusingly 'a hero'). We learn from Beowulf's first speech at

Heorot that Grendel is a 'fierce monster' who eschews weapons and that:

> byreð blodig wæl,    byrgean þenceð,
> *[Grendel] will carry off the bloody corpse, intending to taste it,*
> eteð angenga    unmurnlice
> *the one who goes alone will eat without remorse*

Grendel is solitary, it seems, and cannibalistic and huge, carrying off thirty warriors in the first attack, years ago. In Grendel's attack on Heorot, where Beowulf now lies waiting, additional details are offered that heighten the terror: Grendel breaks off the door of the hall at the lightest touch; he feels immense rage intending to kill all the warriors in Beowulf's troop who are asleep; and from his eyes emanates 'ligge gelicost leoht unfæger' ('an ugly light, most like a flame').

Descriptive detail also continues *after* the fight in Heorot, when Beowulf (himself somewhat monstrous as the strongest of men on earth) recounts his victory not once, but twice—to Hroðgar in the morning, and again to his uncle, King Hygelac, on his return to Geatland. This drip-feeding of detail is surely more frightening than receiving the full picture all at once. We are never quite sure what Grendel really looks like, which provides wonderful opportunities for the imagination—terror's most useful tool—to take over. And just in case we were minded to construct and dismiss him as an outright bedevilled demon, we are introduced to Grendel's mother the night after Beowulf's victory. She is nameless, but comes to seek vengeance for the death of her son, as she should according to the ethos of the Germanic Heroic code.

Elements of humanness and the supernatural, of demonic lineage and familial love combine to create these two troubling and unknowable monsters in *Beowulf*. A third monster—a fifty-foot fire-breathing treasure-hoarding dragon—that finally defeats Beowulf seems less problematic somehow. It might be, then, the proximity of the monstrous to the human that creates the most disruption to the status quo. This would be true geographically, as much as in terms of physical relatedness. The most successful aliens in modern science fiction, whether in books or films, are depicted as human-like with, perhaps, two legs, a body, and a head, and it is their encounters with humans that bring conflict and terror.

## Encountering and transforming

In taking the gamble of travelling into unmapped and potentially untamable spaces, the medieval explorer could not have known what he or she would encounter. From the classical period, at least, when Pliny discussed the strange and wonderful human races in India and Africa, numerous literary works survive that appear to provide orientation for the interested traveller, sharing some of the creatures they describe in common.

These works extend to maps like the glorious and enormous Hereford map of the world, the *Mappa mundi*, the margins of which are filled with the unusual bodies of the peoples that one could hope (or fear) to meet. Audiences can see or hear about people-like races such as the headless Brixontes, whose eyes and mouth are in their chests; the Homodubii, who are humanlike from head to navel and like a donkey from the waist down. The traveller need not fear the Homodubii, because they run away if they see or hear anyone nearby. The Donestre are also part-human, part-animal, and can speak every language known to humankind (see Figure 5); with this linguistic aptitude, they lure the unwary traveller into their trap, and proceed to devour their prey, except for the head, over which the Donestre then weep. Monstrous women—Amazonians (like the race of women defeated by Theseus in Chaucer's *Knight's Tale*)—have distorted bodies, and clearly threaten men with whom they come into contact.

Writers and artists lingered over the depiction of these curiosities. Whole, cogent tales were concocted to provide contexts that

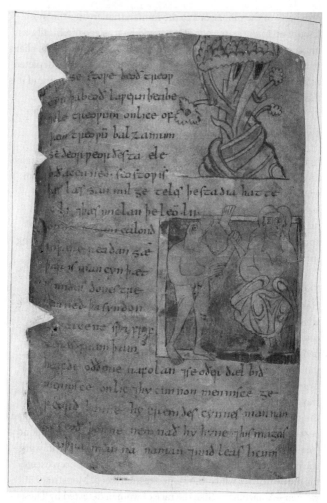

5. *Marvels of the East*, London, British Library, Cotton Vitellius A. xv, folio 103 verso (the *Beowulf*-manuscript Donestre monster).

appeared truthful. The illustrated text called the *Marvels of the East* in the *Beowulf*-manuscript (Figure 5) lists the monsters that one might meet in the region of the Red Sea. An immensely popular narrative, the *Letter of Prester John*, circulated widely in Europe; and in the second half of the 14th century, the French *Book of John Mandeville* appeared, translated into Middle English within decades, as well as Irish, Welsh, Latin, and many other languages. Cast as personal histories with a first-person, eyewitness narrator, these texts are predominantly fictional, but supply numerous geographic and factual elements. Rather like *Alexander to Aristotle* in the *Beowulf* manuscript, and the whole buoyant tradition of *Alexander*-romances, real places, from Europe to India to Egypt, are juxtaposed with fantastical inhabitants to entertain, inform, and simultaneously misinform. They remind medieval audiences of the benefits of being in familiar places as well, contrarily, as whetting the appetite of the adventurous.

Journeys in medieval literature almost always involved discovery. In the real journeys of Gerald of Wales through Wales and through Ireland, he encountered a wide range of people, stories, and curiosities that he was not able to explain. In the questing exploits of great heroes, such as the Arthurian knights, or heroes in nations' originary myths, inexplicable creatures and grotesque characters populate the landscape. In the early Irish Ulster Cycle's *Togail Bruidne Da Derga* (*The Destruction of the Hostel of Da Derga*), Cichuil is a monstrous woman, with enlarged genitals, whose one-eyed, one-footed, and one-handed husband is a swineherd, called Fer Caille. This couple is paralleled by Cymydei Cymeinfoll and Llasar Llaes Gyfnewid, who flee from Ireland to the Welsh court of King Bendigeidfran, carrying the Pair Dadeni (magic cauldron of rebirth), which they present as a gift. This narrative is part of the second branch *Mabinogi of Branwen*, and the numbers of parallel motifs and characters show the close relationship between Irish and Welsh literature—the Celtic tradition.

There is no doubt that the magical or supernatural was thought of as potentially monstrous; elements of the otherworldly with its refusal to comply with the order and familiarity of the real world could also be regarded as threatening and portentous. Indeed, the Latin root of 'monster' is *monstrum*, 'portent, warning, prodigy', and at its simplest and least threatening, the monstrous is someone or something *different* from the norm. In the case of the 14th-century English poem *Sir Orfeo*, the supernatural is very present in the shape of the Otherworld, which breaks into the natural order of the world of Orfeo and his wife, Heroudis. This poem is a Breton lay, a short form of romance, which typically contains elements of the magical and supernatural. It exists in three manuscripts, the earliest of which is Edinburgh, National Library of Scotland, Advocates 19. 2. 1, the Auchinleck Manuscript, dated to *c*.1330 (see Box 8).

This genre of Breton lay derives from the form developed by Marie de France in her late 12th-century French *Lais*, and it may be that a lost French *Lay of Orfeo* influenced the Middle English text. *Sir Orfeo* brilliantly reveals the nature of medieval textual composition through adaptation and transformation. Its inspiration is the story of Orpheus and Eurydice from Ovid's *Metamorphoses*, a myth that also appears in Boethius' *Consolation of Philosophy* (translated in the 9th century by King Alfred and his scholars, and in the 14th by Geoffrey Chaucer), and in Walter Map's *De nugis curialium*. The *Liber monstrorum* contains a reference to Orfeus; and, much later, in the 15th century, Robert Henryson (1460–1500), a Scottish *makar* (a court poet, like the Welsh bards), also writes a verse poem, *Orpheus and Euridice*.

In the traditional Ovidian versions of the myth, which includes Henryson's retelling, Orpheus loses his wife Eurydice to the king of the Underworld, but he wins her back through his superlative harp-playing. However, on exiting the Underworld, he does what the king forbade him to—he looks back at his wife coming behind him—and he loses her forever. In *Sir Orfeo*, Orfeo (now a king

## Box 8  Scottish literature

Scotland has long been a nexus for significant cross-cultural exchange. Originally inhabited by the Picts in the north, in the 5th century, the Scotti (or Gaels), an eastern Irish tribe, settled in the west of Scotland. From the later 8th century, Scandinavian immigration was important; and the influence of the Anglo-Saxons and, subsequently, the French, all played major roles in Scottish culture and literature. Apart from place-names and some Pictish inscriptions, early literature includes the Latin *Life of St Columba*, the Irish saint who founded Iona in 563, whose *Life* was written by Adomnán in the 7th century. Scottish poets also travelled to Ireland to work for royal and ecclesiastical patrons; and early Welsh poetry is also intertwined in the long history of Celtic literature across the British Isles.

This complex network of languages and influences is seen in the 16th-century Book of the Dean of Lismore, a manuscript containing works written in Scots Gaelic, as well as Middle Scots, and Latin. This reflects the vibrant literary culture of Scotland from the 14th century onwards, when English, French, and Latin literature was written and performed in Scotland, beginning, most notably with John Barbour's Middle Scots *Brus*. The 15th century witnessed the emergence of the *makars*, a significant group of court poets writing in English, such as Dunbar and Henryson, whose corpora of work are highly renowned.

with his capital at Winchester) loses his wife to the malevolent Faery King with his Otherworld, which dystopically parallels Orfeo's own kingdom and castle. Orfeo abandons everything and lives as a penitent in the forest with only his harp to remind him of happier days. He sees his wife with the Faeries and follows them back to the Otherworld, where he wins her back by playing his harp. In this story, Eurydice and Orfeo both make it back to Winchester and they resume their life happily after the ten-year hiatus.

This sophisticated, evocative, and engaging poem of just 604 lines intertwines classical myth with contemporary courtly references, a 14th-century setting, and Celtic traditions and superstitions involving Faeries. Influencing the composition of *Sir Orfeo*, as with the medieval *Tristan* stories, are the Irish narratives of the *aithed*, the 'abducted, the taken', where humans were stolen by the Faeries to be left in a sort of limbo state. The depiction of these bodies, lying around the walls of the castle, is monstrous indeed. In *Sir Orfeo*, Orfeo gazes on all manner of people who had been brought to the Otherworld, and who 'seemed dead and yet were not': the headless body; some bodies without arms; some horribly wounded; some bound up in madness; some still armed and sitting on their horses; some strangled while feasting; some drowned; some burnt; some insane; women in the midst of childbirth; and then his own wife, in a still-life, taken as she slept under a magically grafted tree. This is a scene akin to the depictions of the Temples in Chaucer's *Knight's Tale*, where violent images dominate; but here in *Sir Orfeo*, it suggests that behind the most glittering environment, and the most courteous etiquette, lies the monstrous in a continuous backdrop to life's fragile joys.

The rapid transformation of the happy human to this seemingly permanent state of neither one thing nor the other is also, perhaps, its own kind of monstrous event. And within this definition of the monstrous or supernatural we might consider the werewolf, Bisclavret, who, in his human form, is a noble Breton baron in Marie de France's late 12th-century *lai* of that name; and Merlin, the wizard, who is able to transform himself into a variety of guises in the contemporary *Estoire de Merlin*; and other shape-shifters, like the devil who disguises himself as a duke in order to impregnate the mother of Sir Gowther in the 15th-century tail-rhyme poem *Sir Gowther*; as well as Bertilak, the nobleman who hosts Sir Gawain, and then transforms into the Green Knight; and, finally, there is the old hag in Chaucer's *Wife of Bath's Tale* (another Breton lay), who magically becomes a beautiful young woman to please her new husband, forced into marriage with her.

The monstrous takes many forms, including forms with no defined shape, or a mysteriously changeable shape, or a shape that is strange and extraordinary, like the arguing birds in the lively 13th-century avian debate, *The Owl and the Nightingale*. The monstrous—like St Christopher or Bisclavret—need not be demonic. There is a more common tendency, though, especially within a Christian context, for that which is not beautiful to be considered inwardly corrupt and thus outwardly monstrous. In effect, the monstrous becomes, in the hands of Christian ideologues, a tool for suppression; and in the hands of the literature of entertainment, a mechanism for exciting curiosity, but also, conversely, instructing audiences that it's sometimes preferable to want to stay among the people one knows.

# Chapter 6
# Love and longing

## From elegiac to lyric

In the earliest years of the medieval period, a predominantly warrior society was gradually Christianized; heroic and religious verse was composed alongside didactic, encyclopedic, legal, and historical prose and poetry; and the formation of community was paramount. We hear the voices of individuals only rarely, and most commonly then in the elegiac mode, where the major themes are loss, sorrow, and resignation. This is not the classical elegy with its strict metre, but rather a genre with grief at its heart. In the Welsh 9th-century Heledd cycle, for example, Heledd laments the loss of her beloved brother, Cynddylan, focusing on the shrieking eagle flying high above the battleground, looking for his corpse-flesh:

> Eryr Pengwern penngarn llwyt, heno
> *Eagle of Pengwern, grey-crested, tonight*
> aruchel y atleis,
> *its shriek is high,*
> eidic am gic a gereis.
> *eager for flesh I loved.*
>
> Eryr Pengwern penngarn llwyt, heno
> *Eagle of Pengwern, grey-crested, tonight*

aruchel y euan
*its call is high,*
eidic am gic Kynddylan.
*eager for for Cynddylan's flesh.*

Eryr Pengwern penngarn llwyt, heno
*Eagle of Pengwern, grey-crested, tonight*
aruchel y adaf
*its claw is high,*
eidic am gic a garaf.
*eager for flesh I love.*

Left alone to mourn the death of Cynddylan in battle against the English Mercians at Shrewsbury, the controlled sparseness and subtle repetition of the verse serve to emphasize Heledd's grief. The use of the motif of the eagle, a Beast of Battle eager for carrion that flies high and joyful while she is sunk low in mourning, is particularly striking. More typical of the medieval elegy (particularly those uttered by women in a Europe-wide literary tradition called *Frauenlieder*, 'women's songs') is the collapse of time within the narrative of the poem, a collapse that might be said to typify grief and disbelief; here, this is noted only in the movement from the past tense in the first stanza to the present tense in the third stanza, so discreetly signalling the potential endlessness of her love and thus her infinite lament for Cynddylan.

Poems similar to this exist also in Old English, but spoken there by unknown women (*The Wife's Lament, Wulf and Eadwacer*). In these two short poetic works, the contexts of loss are neither explicit nor retrievable, but the searing pain of apparently permanent isolation and anguish is lyrically intense and immediately understood. Other English elegies (*The Wanderer, The Seafarer, The Ruin*) bemoan the loss of a lord or community, and highlight the transience of earthly life by using the *Ubi sunt?* ('Where are they?') motif: 'Where has the horse gone? Where has the man gone?

Where have the treasure-givers gone?' asks the Wanderer, as he moves through a temporal world bereft of all that he has loved.

It is apparent from reading these short poems written down in the 10th century, as well as other texts, that the Anglo-Saxons were thoroughly equipped to write movingly and evocatively using the first person 'I'. However, it is sometimes stated by scholars that 'love', subjectivity, and the concept of individuality are not evident in this earlier literature, which, to a greater or lesser extent, can also be regarded as reflecting the culture that produced it. What creates this response is the contrast between the heroic subject matter of these earlier texts and the romantic focus of many works that are created in the post-Conquest period, after about 1100.

The lyrical voice, it is said, emerges in British and Irish writings with the invention of what is *labelled* the 'lyric', a short poetic form that spread from France throughout Europe in the 12th century. Its main theme was specifically romantic love. The chivalric code replaced the heroic; the courtly replaced the *comitatus*; the lyrical voice took on a life of its own. The lyric might best be described in the words of the 19th-century intellectual John Ruskin as 'the expression by the poet of his own feelings'.

The origin both of the term 'lyric' and its method of composition lies in music; these short poems with a subject-speaker uttering his or her own thoughts and emotions would originally be accompanied by the harp or the lyre. The French itinerant trouvères and troubadours who sought patronage for their compositions not only produced *chansons de geste* and other forms of romance, but also shorter lyrics.

So popular was the form that many hundreds of lyrics survive from throughout the British Isles in all the major languages. These can be categorized broadly as secular; religious—that is, devotional, penitential, moral; and political and satirical. There are multiple varieties of lyric, too, including the *carole* (a joyful song or hymn, which might originally have been danced to), the *pastourelle* (focusing on the countryside, the pastoral), the *reverdie* (a song which celebrates the return of spring), and the *ballade* (three verses each with the same one-line refrain). These new forms of romantic poetry focused on idealizing the service to, and love of, a lady, instead of depicting the love of a warrior for his lord, as with much of the secular poetry previously. Such romantic themes, vocabulary, and imagery could also be deployed effectively and affectively to describe an individual's absolute devotion to the Virgin Mary or Christ.

Lyrics could range widely in terms of subject matter and form. Some of the earliest in English are those of Godric of Finchale, a hermit, who composed three lyrical hymns that were included in his Latin biography by Reginald of Coldingham: the *Libellus de vita et miraculis Sancti Godrici, heremitae de Finchale* (*Book of the Life and Miracles of Saint Godric, hermit of Finchale*). One lyric was sung by Godric to St Nicholas; another was sung *to* Godric by his deceased sister, Burgwine, when she appeared in a vision to reassure him of her salvation.

But lyrics, even ones about death, were not always so spiritually expressed. The late 13th-century Cambridge, Trinity College B. 14. 39 is a collection of over forty works written in English, Latin, and French. It was probably written in western England for a multilingual individual to use in his or her devotions. The short and pithy *When the Turf is your Tower* swiftly deals with life, reminding the reader-listener that this world's joys are worth nothing when we're dead:

> Wen þe turuf is þi tuur,
> *When the turf is your tower,*
> And þi put is þi bour,
> *And the grave is your bedroom*
> Þi wel and þi wite þrote
> *Your skin and your white throat*

Sculen wormes to note.
*Shall be good for the worms.*
Wat helpit þe þenne
*What help for you then will be*
Al þe worilde wunne?
*All the world's joys?*

Here, the direct approach (directed to any reader, but particularly pertinent to an aristocratic woman, concerned about the beauty of her skin and white throat) rather brutally reminds everyone of the imminence and certainty of death. Indeed, many lyrics from the period, echoing the concerns of the preacher in church, are keen to ensure that death, with its attendant horrors, remains in sight, but with a promise of *celestial* joys for those who lead a good, Christian life.

## Love of a lady

In the mid-11th-century English romance *Apollonius of Tyre*, the hero Apollonius falls in love with Arcestrate, a princess, but only once she has made her love for him utterly apparent, declaring: 'I love the shipwrecked man who was betrayed by misadventure; but in case you hesitate about this statement, it is Apollonius, my teacher, that I want.' Arcestrate gets what she most desires; she gets Apollonius. In the copying of this classical romance in Cambridge, Corpus Christi College, 201, the scribe-compiler may well have been reflecting literary and cultural changes that were already under way in England, inspired by Norman influences or French speakers at Edward the Confessor's court. Certainly, by the 12th century, courtly love becomes a major theme in romance and all its associated genres, including hagiography and history.

Courtly love belongs very much to the chivalric ethos, an ideal of nobility and proper knightly behaviour to which the aristocracy aspired. The aristocracy and those committed to the church were the dominant elites from the secular and religious orders, and courtly love had quite an impact on both. The medieval knight had to prove himself as a martial expert; he had also to prove himself emotionally and spiritually. In this idealized, and often nostalgic, world, the inspiration for the knight's determination to test himself and to perform courageously and virtuously came from the love of his chosen lady, whose favour he won through his devotion.

The medieval knight fought and loved for himself, then, as much as for his king and fellow knights. Romances, in particular, were an important genre, entertaining audiences of men and women, but, more significantly, informing them, too. At the court of Henry II and Eleanor of Aquitaine (1154–89), French romances both reflected and contributed to the social and intellectual *mores* of the nobles; the knight owed allegiance and loyalty to his lord *and* to his lady, to whom, in addition, he was to promise complete obedience.

The love that emerged from this relationship between a knight and his lady was the purest love: *fin'amor* (or *fine amor*). It brought about an exaltation of the lovers, and especially a bettering of the knight, but its loss or diminution was devastating. This topos of suffering for love results in the transformation of the lovesick that can be so devastating as to cause their appearance to alter dramatically, or can even bring about death. The legend of Tristan and Iseut, which may have been influenced by earlier Irish legends, was written in French in the second half of the 12th century. Two versions that now exist only in fragmentary form were composed: one by Beroul; the other, a more courtly version, by Thomas of Britain. The narrative proved to have wide appeal, and it was translated into prose, and into many different languages, including Middle English and Welsh.

Tristan and Iseut's is a story that questions the ideal of romantic love in relation to the realities of aristocratic life. In the poetic version of the story, Tristan is a knight sent to Ireland to bring Iseut back to marry his uncle, Mark, king of Cornwall. Tristan and Iseut fall in love with each other after drinking a potion, but even so, Iseut marries Mark and continues her relationship with Tristan. Mark eventually finds out and determines to execute the lovers, but Tristan manages to save himself and rescue Iseut and they escape, eventually returning and making peace with Mark. Tristan marries a different Lady Iseut in Brittany, but swears to maintain chastity in that marriage.

One day, when he is severely wounded, he calls for his original Iseut to come and heal him, but his wife lies and tells him she did not come. He dies of sorrow; and the first Iseut, who arrives too late, dies too. Their union in death is their final respite in Thomas of Britain's version, written in octosyllabic rhyming couplets:

> Embrace le, si s'estent,
> *She embraces and stretches out by him,*
> baise li la buche e la face,
> *kisses his mouth and his face,*
> e molt estreit a li l'enbrace.
> *and holds him tightly to her.*
> Cors a cors, buche a buche estent,
> *Body to body, mouth to mouth she lies,*
> sun spirit a itant rent,
> *she renders up her spirit now*
> e murt dejuste lui iussi
> *and, in this way next to him, dies*
> pur la dolur de sun ami.
> *for sorrow of her friend.*

It's easy to read swiftly through the sequence of movements leading to the double death here. But the actions, which would be sexual in another context (embracing, lying next to, kissing, holding tightly, body to body, mouth to mouth), are profoundly sad and moving: she clings to the corpse of her life's love. That the only resolution for the adulterous courtly lovers is death is a worrying message, perhaps. Yet the all-consuming and absolute love Tristan and Iseut share has its own tragic nobility evoked in this scene, especially, in their embrace of death. The story's popularity, too, illustrates how much it engaged writers and audiences, including Marie de France, who retold part of it in her *lai Chevrefoil*.

Within the many lyrics that survive, the romance heroine features often as the subject of male desire. Dafydd ap Gwilym, the noble Welsh bard writing in the mid-14th century, poured out his love for the married Morfudd in a sequence of poems. In *Morfudd fel yr Haul* (*Morfudd like the Sun*), he describes her as his 'pure girl', his 'dazzling girl', his 'noble, clever girl', his 'darling', 'the procurer of May', but her beauty is also a 'golden web'; she is deceitful, a trickster, and beyond his reach. She brings the spring, when all thoughts turn to love and procreation (and anticipation of the fun of the pilgrimage, as Chaucer tells us in the opening of *The Canterbury Tales*). 'Gŵyr obryn serchgerdd o'm pen', Dafydd ap Gwilym proclaims: 'She knows how to get a love song from my lips.' This, and many other, poets' love is not always so courtly, though. In *Y Rhugl Groen* (*The Rattle Bag*), he tell us he is in the middle of 'conferring' with a girl 'dan wŷdd rhwng mynydd a maes' ('under green trees between mountain and meadow') after some mead and, to his extreme annoyance, their intercourse is interrupted by a shepherd with a rattle bag and the girl runs away.

In numerous other lyrics, the sexuality of women forms the main focus of the male viewers' obsession, especially when spring arrives. London, British Library, Harley 2253, a manuscript written in about 1340 (see Figure 6), contains 116 Latin, French, and English texts, among them a whole host of lyrics that represent the full range of possibilities of the form: religious, secular, penitential, moral, and political. Many of these texts in Harley 2253 centre on women. Four ribald French *fabliaux*, such as *Le Chevalier qui fist les cuns parler* (*The Knight who Makes Cunts Talk*), use romance diction and themes, but in a bawdy and explicitly misogynistic sexual context, like Chaucer's *Reeve's Tale*.

**6. London, British Library, Harley 2253, folio 71 verso.**

Less overtly anti-feminist, in the English *Alysoun*, the poet sings
to the heroine mentioning her brown eyebrows, lovely
countenance, and tiny waist, declaring that he will die if he cannot
have her, before launching into a trite refrain. In *Advice to Women*,

the poet warns women that when spring returns, women should beware of men, who just want their money and virginity. Women's beauty and desirability dominates these secular lyrics, creating of them objects to be worshipped, but also possessed and subdued.

## Speaking of love

One of the most beautiful and complex female lovers is Criseyde in Chaucer's *Troilus and Criseyde*, written in the 1380s (see Figure 3). Using Boccaccio's *Il filostrato* as a source, and inspired by the classical Ovid and later, medieval writers, Chaucer dramatically, but respectfully, adapts his *auctoritees* ('authorities') to provide a lively and compelling narrative. Chaucer sets his great love story in ancient Troy at the time of the Siege of Troy, though this is a Troy re-envisioned as a bustling medieval London.

In the five books that comprise this lengthy masterpiece, Chaucer sustains over 8,000 lines of Rhyme Royal stanzas (lines with five metrical feet in stanzas of seven lines, rhyming ababbcc). This is the story of love, and of truth in love, a story of the constancy of God's love that endures beyond the whims of fortune, and human separation, loss, and death. Troilus struck by the god of love falls deeply in love with the young widow, Criseyde, and instantly feels the pain that accompanies desire:

> 'If no love is, O god, what fele I so?
> *If love it's not, O God, what feel I so?*
> And if love is, what thing and whiche is he?'
> *And if love it is, what sort of thing is it?'*

The lovers' physical union is aided by Criseyde's uncle and Troilus' confidant, Pandarus, but then Criseyde is sent to the Greek camp, where she pledges herself to another man, despite promising Troilus that she would return to him. When she does not come back, Troilus throws himself into battle, and is killed by Achilles. In the eighth sphere (a sort of ancients' heaven), Troilus realizes that love's permanence is not achieved in mortal things, even though loving is part of human nature. Chaucer closes his love story with tender reminders of the beauty of love in both its physical and spiritually redemptive qualities:

> O yonge fresshe folkes, he or she,
> *O young fresh people, he or she,*
> In which that love up groweth with your age,
> *In whom love grows as you get older,*
> Repeyreth hoom from worldly vanitee,
> *Come home from worldly vanity,*
> And of your herte up-casteth the visage
> *And cast up your heart's countenance*
> To thilke god that after his image
> *To that same God who in his own image*
> Yow made; and thinketh al nis but a fayre
> *Made you; and think all is but a market-place*
> This world, that passeth sone as floures fayre.
> *In this world, that passes as quickly as fair flowers.*

Chaucer's emphasis at the end of his poem on the naturalness and beauty of love ('yonge fresshe folkes', 'floures fayre') results in a positive depiction of love. This is despite the ostensible illicitness of Troilus and Criseyde's consummation of their love, and despite Criseyde's inability to keep her promise. Troilus' ascent to a place where he can discern that all earthly things are transient confirms the potential joy of capacious love.

It seems that this same message of love's magnificence and its redemptive qualities underpins Sir Thomas Malory's depiction of his greatest lovers, Lancelot and Guinevere. The story of King Arthur, Queen Guinevere, the Knights of the Round Table and the Quest for the Holy Grail is told in the magnificent 15th-century romance *Le Morte Darthur*, completed, Malory reveals, while he was a 'knight prisoner' in 1469, during the turmoil of the Wars of the Roses.

Basing some of his twenty-one-book prose narrative on earlier English and French authorities, Malory makes this tragic tale of chivalry, loyalty, private love, guilt, and public shame entirely his own. He chooses not only English as his medium, but also the gravitas of prose to underscore the 'historical' nature of his expansive and fast-moving story. Through realistic dialogue, Malory depicts the love between Lancelot and Guinevere as noble, for, in courtly love, the most worthy knight can surely only love the most noble lady. When discovered by Mordred and other knights, who aim to publicly accuse the lovers of treason, Lancelot touchingly sums up his loyalty and his hope for salvation through Guinevere's intercession:

> Then he took the queen in his arms, and kissed her, and said: 'Most noble Christian queen, I beseech you as ye have been ever my special good lady, and I at all times your true poor knight unto my power, and as I never failed you in right nor in wrong sithen the first day King Arthur made me knight, that ye will pray for my soul if that I here be slain…'

It is not Lancelot who is slain ultimately, but Arthur, whose death is the result of the war caused by Mordred's public demand for retribution against Lancelot. And while Guinevere is Lancelot's 'earthly joy', penance is required for the downfall of Arthur's kingdom brought about by their love. Both take up a religious life to seek perfection and atone for the death of Arthur. The heartbreaking final books of *Le Morte Darthur* recount the deaths of Guinevere and Lancelot: she 'peerless', and he 'the courteost knight', 'the truest friend', the 'meekest', the 'gentlest', the 'sternest'.

## Love of the lord and lady

This spiritual aspect of love was not new in the 14th and 15th centuries. The 12th century brought about innovation in spiritual devotion that was closely allied with the emergence of romantic love. There is a new articulation and appreciation of the individual's relationship with fellow humans and with God and the community of saints. In the later medieval period, poignant images of Christ's suffering and his broken body begin to dominate artistic and literary depictions. The anguish of his mother, Mary, features prominently, too. By focusing on the heartache and wounds of these holy figures, authors and artists sought to engender in their audiences a desire to emulate and venerate Jesus and Mary's spiritual perfection; a desire that the faithful Christian learn to love wholly.

Romance imagery and diction were appropriated for spiritual work. Language that might be associated with a courtly woman was adapted for the Virgin Mary; the pleading courtly lover was transformed into the penitent worshipper. The 13th-century lyric from Cambridge, Trinity College, B. 14. 39, *Of One That is So Fair and Bright*, demonstrates the flexibility of language and the expected multilingualism of a well-educated medieval reader-listener. It is written in macaronic verse; that is, verse that moves between languages while maintaining all rhetorical effects. Here the meaning of a verse-line of English is expanded and enhanced by the short Latin prayer-like verse-line that follows:

> For on þat is so feir ant brist
> *Of one that is so fair and bright*
> Velud maris stella,
> *Like the star of the sea,*
> Bristore þen þe daiis list,
> *Brighter than the day's light,*
> Parens et puella,
> *Mother and maiden;*
> I crie þe grace of þe.
> *I cry to you for grace from you.*
> Levedi, priie þi sone for me,
> *Lady, pray to your son for me,*

Tam pia,
*So holy,*
Þat I mote come to þe,
*That I might come to you,*
Maria.

This personal plea to a beautiful, holy Virgin Mary, who is asked
to intercede for the penitent, anticipates the deep love between
the supplicant and the saint. This personal love, expressed in
the first-person 'I' to draw in all reader-listeners, has its most
magnificent appearance in English surprisingly early, in the
10th-century *Dream of the Rood*, which details, over 156 lines, the
entirety of salvation history, with a focus on its crux, the redemption
of mankind through Christ's crucifixion. When the visionary sees
an immeasurable cross in the sky above, covered in gold, adored by
creation, his or her response is adoration suffused with contrition:
'Syllic wæs se sigebeam ond Ic synnum fah' ('Glorious was the tree
of victory and I stained with sins'). This tightly controlled verse-line,
dense with profound theological complexity, juxtaposes glory with
sin (through the <s> alliteration) to highlight that the sinner can be
saved from their horrific position through recognition of the victory
of Christ over the Devil.

The ability of the visionary to participate in potential salvation
through contemplation of and empathy with Christ and Mary's
suffering is evinced most dramatically in the mystical writings that
*The Dream of the Rood* heralds. These reach their apogee in the
14th- and 15th-century works of Walter Hilton (1340–96, who
wrote *The Scale of Perfection*); the anonymous author of *The Cloud
of Unknowing*; the Yorkshire hermit Richard Rolle (*c*.1290–1349);
the anchoress Julian of Norwich (*c*.1342–1416); and the pilgrim
and visionary Margery Kempe (*c*.1373–1439).

Mysticism involves a loving intimacy with Christ, dependent on
sustained meditative focus in order to begin to attain spiritual
union with God. It is a tradition that can be traced back to the

earliest period in church history through the writings of major theologians. In the High Middle Ages, though, its practitioners were sometimes secular and, notably, female. Mystical Christianity emphasizes an emotional bond with God and the saints that insists on an affective piety, a fervent pious response that is inspired by reflecting hard on the sufferings of Christ in his humanity.

The language adopted in uttering this relationship is often sensual, reminiscent of romantic love in its yearning and desire. Rolle says, in his *Ego dormio*, written in the 1340s:

> Jhesu, Jhesu, Jhesu, til þe it es þat I morne,
> *Jesus, Jesus, Jesus, it is for you that I mourn,*
> For my lyfe and my lyvyng, when may I hethen torne?
> *Because, my life and my living, when can I return there [to you]?*
> Jhesu, my dere and my drewry, delyte ert þou to synge;
> *Jesus, my dear and my bounty, delight are you to sing;*
> Jhesu, my myrth, my melody, when will þow cum, my Keyng?
> *Jesus, my mirth, my melody, when will you come, my king?*
> Jhesu, my hele and my hony, my whart and my comfortyng,
> *Jesus, my help and my honey, my health and my comforting,*
> Jhesu, I covayte forto dy when it es þi payng.
> *Jesus, I covet death when it is your pleasing.*

This zealous love demanding the frequent repetition of the lover's name is touching and clearly overwhelming for the speaker. *The Book of Margery Kempe*, dictated to a scribe-editor in the 15th century by the 'creature', as she calls herself, reveals in the *Proem* how overwhelming she found her contemplation and envisioning of Christ: 'Sche knew and undyrstod many secret and prevy thyngys...And often tymes, while sche was kept wyth swech holy spechys and dalyawns, sche schuld so wepyn and sobbyn þat many men wer gretly awondyr, for thei wysten ful lytyl how homly ower Lord was in hyr sowle.' ('She knew and understood many secret and private things...And oftentimes, while she was kept with such holy speeches and conversations [with Jesus], she would weep and sob so that many people were greatly amazed, because they knew very little about how at home the Lord was in her soul.') Margery points out the surprised reaction of those around her, and that was the mildest of responses that she received. She became quite notorious in her daily life and her travels, as she tells us, and she sought spiritual advice from the highly regarded female mystic Julian of Norwich.

Julian's own work, *Revelations of Divine Love* (written down in the 1390s), describes her visions of Christ and his Passion, focusing on the divine love that she saw as underpinning everything. In a tenet for all time she wrote (chapter 27):

> In my folly, afore this time often I wondered why by the great foreseeing wisdom of God the beginning of sin was not letted: for then, methought, all should have been well. This stirring was much to be forsaken, but nevertheless mourning and sorrow I made therefor, without reason and discretion.

> But Jesus, who in this Vision informed me of all that is needful to me, answered by this word and said: 'It behoved that there should be sin; but all shall be well, and all shall be well, and all manner of thing shall be well.'

It is this promise of all being well that encouraged many to strive for salvation despite war, plague, famine, and injustice, and that inspired writers to seek to save themselves and those for whom they wrote.

# Chapter 7
# Death and judgement

## Desiring salvation

Chaucer's *Retraction*, or *Retracciouns*, is appended to *The Parson's Tale*, the final text in *The Canterbury Tales*. Immediately before the *Retraction*, the scribe tells the reader-listener that Chaucer has finished his *Tales*: 'Heere taketh the makere of this book his leve.' Chaucer then talks directly to his audience, advising them that if there is anything among his writings that they like, they should thank the Lord Jesus, but that if there is something that displeases them or that might be considered offensive, they attribute it to Chaucer's lack of knowledge, not his deliberate intent:

> And if ther be any thyng that displese hem, I preye hem also that they arrete it to the defaute of myn unkonnynge and nat to my wyl, that wolde ful fayn have seyd bettre if I hadde had konnynge. For oure book seith, 'Al that is writen is writen for oure doctrine', and that is myn entente…Lord Jhesu Crist…sende me grace to biwayle my giltes and to studie to the salvacioun of my soule…

> *And if there's anything that displeases them, I pray also that they'll attribute it to the fault of my ignorance and not to my will, and that I'd have said better if I had had the ability. For our book says, 'All that is written is written for our doctrine', and that is my intention…Lord Jesus Christ…send me grace to lament my sins and to meditate upon the salvation of my soul…*

The *Retraction* actually names books that Chaucer seeks to revoke, among them the romance *Troilus and Criseyde*, the *Book of the Duchess*, and those of the *Canterbury Tales* 'that sownen into synne' ('that tend toward sin'). The translation of Boethius' *Consolation of Philosophy* (the *Boece*), the hagiographies, sermons, moral, and devotional writings that Chaucer wrote should, he tells us, be considered as lending him grace to hope for the salvation of his soul.

Importantly, this confessional statement immediately follows the moral and penitential *Parson's Tale*. The Parson delivers this long prose tale just outside Canterbury at the end of the pilgrims' journey from London during which many of the varied and lively pilgrims have told their tales. Chaucer has taken pains to narrate all the tales of the pilgrims precisely, according to the exact words they used. Since they are from many different classes and walks of life (from the Knight to the Ploughman, Wife of Bath to the Prioress, Squire to Summoner), his audience has been entertained with tales appropriate to the tellers: bawdy *fabliaux* juxtaposed with romance; saints' lives; beast fables; sermons; and moral exempla. Now, it appears in the *Retraction* that Chaucer worries for his soul, though given how naive and tongue-in-cheek Chaucer's narrator-persona has been in the course of *The Canterbury Tales*, many scholars doubt the earnestness of this short coda.

It is difficult to tell whether or not Chaucer was genuine in his stated desire for salvation and his concern about his work's potential for leading audiences into sin. Many other authors in the medieval period intervened in their texts to request forgiveness or beseech their audience's prayers (Augustine, Bede, Denis Piramus in his 12th-century French *Life of St Edmund*, Gerald of Wales), suggesting that this act was something of a literary device. But, while at the least such an action might be authors hedging their bets, it seems equally possible that a summative statement asking for grace and salvation would be genuine, given how pervasive Christianity was in the British Isles throughout this period, and how immersed in it individuals were.

Centuries earlier, Cynewulf, the 9th- or 10th-century author of Old English religious and hagiographic poetry, gave his name in runes towards the end of his *Fates of the Apostles*. By doing this, he writes himself into the poem about the acts of Christ's disciples, and becomes the last name in the catalogue of apostles. He also makes himself known to his audience, and explicitly seeks his audience's assistance in finding comfort and salvation, just as Chaucer seeks grace and the hope of salvation from Christ, Mary, and the saints.

Similarly, the Welsh author Meilyr Brydydd who was poet to Gruffydd ap Cynan, the prince of Gwynedd, begins his beautiful thirty-eight-line *Marwysgafn Feilyr Brydydd* ('Deathbed Song') with a Latin exhortation to God beseeching the recognition of his true Lord:

> *Rex Regum*, rhebydd rhwydd Ei foli,
> *King of kings, lord easy to praise,*
> I'm arglwydd uchaf archaf weddi:
> *I ask this prayer of my highest lord:*
> Gwledig gwlad orfod goruchel wenrod,
> *Country-conquering ruler of the best and holy land,*
> Gwrda, gwna gymod rhyngod a mi.
> *Noble lord, make peace between you and me.*

These declarations suggest that a lifetime's writing, and especially the very act of writing deeply religious works, could be sufficient to inspire the writer spiritually. Writing and its performance—as in the mystical corpus of texts—could transform the individual from a state of sinfulness to a state of grace.

## Preaching salvation

From the earliest days of the church in the 1st century, teaching the basic tenets of belief and preaching God's word to the assembled were the fundamental responsibilities of those in religious orders.

Indeed, the success of Christianity in the conversion period and later (6th century onwards) depended on the provision of books and texts from which preachers and teachers could instruct and evangelize. As such, religious poetry and prose, including materials specifically designed for use in church services, dominate all other kinds of textual production through the first sixteen or seventeen centuries of Christianity.

Most ecclesiastical institutions with access to a scribe, even indirectly (and many had whole teams of scribes), had copies of liturgical books used by bishops, monks, nuns, and priests to assist them in officiating services and sacraments; and patristic writings from which those in holy orders studied and drew inspiration. Abbots, abbesses, bishops, and priors delivered sermons to the brothers and sisters in the abbey or convent, sometimes in Latin; or, at other times, in one of the vernaculars. Ralph D'Escures, early 12th-century Archbishop of Canterbury, reveals that he delivered sermons to his monks in French first, before having them transcribed into Latin for a more public delivery.

The majority of texts that survive, then, are sermons and saints' lives, composed, copied, adapted, and sometimes memorized to be delivered in the language or dialect appropriate to the specific part of the British Isles, or specific institutional context. Writers often used and reused parts of earlier existing works, and cited (or mis-cited) authoritative sources, like Augustine, Bede, or Gregory the Great, to validate and elevate their work among fellow religious and parishioners.

Within the many hundreds of parishes, everyone was supposed to attend church, though perhaps many were not as regular in their churchgoing as the church wished. At many points in their lives, the average parishioner would hear the homiletic and hagiographic literature produced for Sundays and feast-days, and this could be poetry, as well as prose. Here, one thinks particularly of the work of a writer like the Augustinian canon Orm, who wrote the

*Ormulum*, a 19,000-line English cycle of verse homilies (a homily explains a scriptural verse, whereas a sermon instructs or admonishes), in the last third of the 12th century; or, arguably, William Langland, whose great 14th-century dream vision, *Piers Plowman*, exemplifies, in brilliant alliterative verse, many homiletic characteristics, and includes within its narrative sermons delivered by allegorical characters trying to teach the assembled crowds.

The writer-speaker sought to bring the faithful to a greater grace; or to convince the sinner to repent; or to encourage the doubtful and exhausted member of the congregation to hope and strive harder for God in their thoughts, words, and deeds. Many collections of sermons survive from the earlier medieval period, testifying to the essential requirement for these texts. They survive particularly in Latin, but also in nearly all other languages of the period; and extant books of sermons increase dramatically from the 13th century.

By the 13th century, preaching was just one tool in a renewed programme of religious instruction initiated by the Catholic church at the Third and Fourth Lateran Councils in 1179 and 1215 that focused on tackling sin, encouraging confession and penitence, and enhancing Christian education. The Fourth Lateran Council, in particular, tried to improve education within the church. In its Clause 22, the Council made the annual confession and taking of communion mandatory for every Christian. As we shall see, this inspired the most prolific composition and dissemination of confessional manuals and pastoral guides for centuries to come and this literature was often then adapted into the form of sermons.

Sermons might not appear to be the most engaging of literature, but a great sermon writer entertained, educated, and motivated his audience. A host of rhetorical devices was used to organize and elucidate essential doctrine, and useful exempla were employed to make the teaching memorable. Poetry in the vernacular could appear in the middle of Latin instruction; handbooks teaching preachers how to write circulated widely; *artes praedicandi*—the art of preaching—was a major concern for clerical writers. New religious orders, like the Friars—both Franciscan and Dominican (founded in 1209 and 1214, respectively)—engaged in pastoral work in Britain and Ireland from the 13th century onwards.

Friars were particularly renowned for the excellence and variety of their mandated preaching, and many small multilingual books survive that seem to have been made for and used by Franciscan friars, particularly; one such manuscript, London, British Library, Harley 913, produced in Ireland in the first half of the 14th century, contains verse sermons, didactic poems and lyrics, and *The Land of Cockayne*, an English poem that satirizes the monastic life through its depiction of a topsy-turvy world. And Oxford, Bodleian Library, Rawlinson poet. 241, a later 13th-century anthology is typical of many manuscripts of this period that contain Latin and French sermons and poems, with the odd smattering of English verse. In medieval books, then, genre was not always as clearly categorized as it tends to be nowadays. Scribes and editors of texts often brought together all the kinds of materials that were needed for the books' users to go about their work in the community.

## Punishing and persecuting

... wearð þes þeodscipe swyþe forsyngod þurh mænigfealde synna and þurh fela misdæda: þurh morðdæda and þurh mandæda, þurh gitsunga and þurh gifernessa, þurh stala and þurh strudunga...

*... this nation has become very sinful through various sins and through many misdeeds: through deadly sins and through crimes, through avarice and through greediness, through theft and pillaging...*

So Wulfstan of York, contemporary of Ælfric, thundered in his 1014
*Sermo lupi ad Anglos* (*Sermon of the Wolf to the English*) to an
assembled congregation of nobles and prelates: 'the nation has
become sinful', 'let us *often* consider the great judgement to which
we must all come, and eagerly defend ourselves against the boiling
fire of hell-torment'.

The idea of perpetual torment in hell was a real fear, confirmed for
congregations throughout the Middle Ages by the fist-banging
exhortatory sermons they would have heard on occasion, and by
the images of suffering souls painted onto church walls. The Fourth
Lateran Council's insistence on confession made the emphasis on
sinfulness and repentance particularly notable. God's anger at
the sins of the nation became evident at times of famine, plague,
civil war, illness, and obvious social injustice; these terrible events
were present throughout the medieval period, and none more so
than in the 13th to 15th centuries.

Fear of death and what would come afterwards, especially for
the sinner, haunted writers throughout this period. In sermons,
preachers dwelled on the horrors of hell. Certain categories of
hell were especially reserved for particular sins: liars are told
they will stand for all eternity up to their necks in excrement
while chewing off their own tongues which are regurgitated
whole, and so it goes on. Murderers, gluttons, and fornicators
have pertinent punishments. All will be dragged by demons into
the mouth of hell on Judgement Day. On the pageant-wagons of
later medieval and early modern drama, hellmouth (through
which all sinners entered hell) appeared as a monstrous face
entertainingly accompanied by smoke and flames and deliberate
chaos, and through which devils poured out uproariously into the
attendant crowd.

In *Body and Soul* texts (sometimes depicted as dreams experienced
by a living narrator), which exist in all languages in this period, the

Soul—knowing that Judgement Day will not go well for it—berates the dead Body for its lack of restraint in life. The Body for its part blames the failures of the Soul as the superior spiritual authority. The 15th-century *Leabhar Breac* (Dublin, Royal Irish Academy, 23 P 16) contains such a debate in Middle Irish, exemplifying an Irish tradition that was highly influential. In a lively encounter between the distressed Soul (who has seen what its eternal punishment will be) and the Body, the Soul shrieks:

'A choland chruaid, a thempuil diabuil, a tégdais dub dorcha dona diabulda, a thopur brén, a chuli chrum, a chiste comthinoil cech pheccaid.'

'O stubborn body, temple of the devil, black, black, miserable, devilish abode, stinking well, nest of worms, treasure of the collection of every sin.'

This extraordinary attack goes on to detail the decay of the body, 'abode of the black-blue beetles', the soul berating the body for the torture it now receives among the devils. The Body fights back, excoriating the Soul ('you stinking puddle, you noose leading captive the body at the instigation of the devil') for not receiving God's word. The preacher, presumably revelling in this brilliant, dramatic dialogue, makes sharp the contrast between the dark hellish eternity of the damned, and the 'melody of song, with quiring of angels' that will meet the saved.

Such dynamic depiction of the effects of sin extended to the dramatization of the sins themselves, which in sermons and poems were often personified to tremendous effect. In *Piers Plowman*, Passus V (the fifth part of Langland's 14th-century dream vision sequence), the audience is shown the most magnificent procession of the Seven Deadly Sins, each portrayed satirically as if a member of contemporary society. Sir Gluttony is shown with Clement the Cobbler and Betty the Butcher in the pub eating, drinking, laughing, and singing:

And seten so til evensong, and songen umwhile
*And they sat like that until it was time for Evensong, and they sung*
*    for a while*
Til Gloton hadde glubbed a galon and a gille.
*Until Glutton had glugged a gallon and a gill.*
His guttes bigonne to goþelen as two gredy sowes;
*His guts began to rumble like two greedy sows';*
He pissed a potel in a Paternoster-while,
*And he pissed a pot-full in the time it takes to say the 'Our Father'*
And blew his rounde ruwet at his ruggebones ende...
*And he blew his round trumpet at his arse end ...*
...And whan he drouȝ to þe dore, þanne dymmed hise eiȝen;
*And when he got close to the door, then his eyes dimmed;*
He thrumbled on þe þresshfold and þrew to þe erþe.
*He stumbled on the threshold and fell to the ground.*
Clement þe Cobelere kauȝte hym by þe myddel
*Clement the Cobbler caught him by the middle*
For to liften hym olofte, and leyde hym on his knowes.
*And lifted him up, and laid him on this knees,*
Ac Gloton was a gret cherl and a grym in þe liftyng,
*But Gluttony was a huge churl and a grim thing in lifting,*
And kouȝed up a cawdel in Clementes lappe.
*And he threw up a mess in Clement's lap.*

On the one hand, this is hilarious; on the other, it is disgusting and repellent, wasteful and careless. The hilarity, though, is sharply undercut by the reminders of what these Sins should be doing: attending Evensong service at church, instead of sitting in the pub all day into the evening; and *saying* the *Pater Noster* in search for forgiveness, rather than pissing and farting grotesquely. Moreover, gluttony was widely regarded as a cause of the Fall of Man, when Eve greedily took the apple in Eden. Even Chaucer's corrupt Pardoner begins his sermon-tale with the exclamation 'O glotonye, full of cursedness! | O cause first of our confusion!'

In addition to the use of sermons and didactic poetry for teaching, terrifying, and offering the means of salvation for audiences, the church and secular state sought to suppress sinful and anti-social behaviour through lawcodes, lay and ecclesiastical, and by confession to a priest followed by instruction. Confessionals and Penitentials that detailed sins and penances circulated in the early medieval period, and Irish influence on these tracts was particularly significant. Penitential acts from prayer to pilgrimage were always important, but after the Fourth Lateran Council in 1215, greater efforts were made to educate the laity to ensure at least they know their *Pater noster*, *Ave Maria*, and Creed. Manuscripts throughout the High Middle Ages contain these texts, often written as marginal additions to major texts in order to prompt the pastor in his work.

Numerous treatises in the later 12th and 13th centuries were written, too, that helped churchmen perform confession and teach their parishioners. These were widely circulated throughout the country. Gerald of Wales's *Gemma ecclesiastica* helped rural churchmen in their duties. Thomas of Chobham's *Summa confessorum* and William de Montibus' poetic *Peniteas cito peccator* are early examples of how to understand and conduct confession, and ensure its efficacy. St Edmund of Abingdon's French *Le Merure de Seinte Eglise* had a big impact, as did William of Pagula's *Oculum sacerdotis*; Guillaume Peyraut's *Summa de vitiis et virtutibus*; and another Dominican, Lorens D'Orléans's French *Somme le roi*, written in 1279. Many of these Latin and French treatises were subsequently translated into English and other languages. The 14th-century *Book of Vices and Virtues* derived from *Somme le roi*; and Dan Michael's prose *Ayenbit of Inwit* (*Remorse of Conscience*), written in 1340 also used the French treatise as its main source. Dan Michael reveals

Þet þis boc is ywrite mid Engliss of Kent;
*That this book is written with English of Kent;*

> Þis boc is ymad vor lewede men,
> *This book is made for unlearned people,*
> Vor vader and vor moder and vor oþer ken.
> *For a father and a mother and for other kin.*

By making Latin confessional and penitential literature available in French, English, and, to a lesser extent, the other British and Irish vernaculars, the 'lewed', the non-clerical Christian would be encouraged to help themselves: to learn how to reflect on and repent for their sins; and how to engage with basic doctrine. Dan Michael's *Ayenbit* might not have been as popular as he intended, given that it only survives in one manuscript copy, but other works survive in multiple copies, attesting to their wide dissemination.

A late 14th-century manual of basic doctrinal instruction, *The Lay Folks' Catechism*, exists in almost thirty manuscript versions with a wide geographical spread. It is associated with the instructional programme of Archbishop Thoresby of York, which itself built on earlier similar injunctions and helped pave the way for a sustained vernacular theology. Certainly, the translation into English meant a broader audience could access the learning it contains. The *Catechism*, in its many forms, and like so many other works in Latin and French in the 13th to 15th centuries, seeks to enumerate the most elementary parts of the Christian faith: the Ten Commandments; the Seven Deadly Sins; the Seven Acts of Mercy; the Seven Virtues; the Seven Sacraments; and the Fourteen Articles of Faith. These fundamental aspects of religious practice were reinforced by whole cycles of wall paintings, such as that in Hoxne Church in Suffolk, which dynamically illustrates the Seven Sins and Seven Acts of Mercy in adjacent paintings on the wall of the nave. This made religious learning, in essence at least, accessible to all in ways that Latin services and priestly mediation did not always facilitate.

## From superstition to persecution

Not all religious or religious-like practice was condoned by the Catholic church; not all converts to Christianity in the early period were thoroughly convinced. The wonderful Old English heroic poem *The Wanderer* details the lonely existence of a warrior without a lord, a man without friends or family. It is focused on the inexorability of fate, the capriciousness of fortune, expressing loss and nostalgia in an apparently unremittingly hopeless monologue until its final line and a half, where the poet suddenly recognizes that his hope lies in focusing on the stability of heaven and the grace of God. Good outcomes could often be attributed to fate, or to the intercession of a saint, but were also assisted by charms or textual amulets. Charms exist to ward off dwarfs, infection, and cysts. Protection was sought when setting out on a journey, and to assist against the loss of property. These charms are often copied into manuscripts that probably have an ecclesiastical origin, and it is difficult for modern scholars to determine what might have been the relationship between orthodox religious practices and what we'd commonly regard as 'superstition' now.

There existed in popular religion a kind of authorized superstition that amounted to promulgating a knowledge of good and bad omens; or using days of the week or patterns of weather to forecast the future ('prognostications' that had a lengthy and established textual tradition); or warding off a potentially terrible childbirth by wearing an amulet with a bit of the *Passion of St Margaret* in it. There was, though, a thin line between this and practices that were outrightly condemned by the church to the point of persecution and attempts at eradication. Even fiction-writing could be regarded suspiciously (which might have contributed towards Chaucer's *Retraction*). The noise of minstrelsy could, according to Robert Mannyng of Brunne in his 14th-century manual, *Handlyng Synne*, result in the minstrel's death through divine retribution, if the minstrel 'desturbled the bensoun | And the gode mannys devocyoun' (disturbed the prayers and the good man's devotions'). Tournaments, miracle plays, and frivolous things were also breeding grounds for sin, and warned against by instructional texts. But the greatest danger was not to be a Christian at all, or to be a Christian with beliefs and practices that differed from those propagated by the central channels of the church.

In fictional romances which idealized the chivalric code and the love of the knight for his lady, the stereotypical antagonist was often the Saracen, the Muslim. This figure was sometimes depicted as noble, able to be converted to Christianity; sometimes depicted as demonic, bestialized, orientalized, and overcome by the hero. Most vitriol in all texts—religious or secular—was saved for the heretic and the Jew. In Ælfric's 10th-century *Passion of St Edmund*, based on Abbo of Fleury's Latin *Passio Sancti Edmundi*, Ælfric specifically condemns the wolf-like, slaughterous Viking killers of Edmund, claiming that they are 'united with the devil', and deliberately associating them with the Jews who killed Jesus.

This idea of the Jews as killers of Christ led to increasing levels of persecution as the Middle Ages progressed, culminating in their expulsion from England in 1290 by royal edict. Allied to this terrible act, the frequent anti-Semitism of medieval writers extended to narrating stories of the Jews as killers of Christian children: the 'blood libel'. The monk Thomas of Norwich wrote a large Latin *Life and Miracles of St William of Norwich*, completed in the 1170s, and told the story of a young boy who, it was alleged, was ritually murdered by the Jews of the city. A similar story appears in Chaucer's *Canterbury Tales*, when the Prioress tells a tale that is unremittingly anti-Semitic, reflecting a very problematic aspect of medieval culture that demands a modern audience's judicious scrutiny and thoughtful approach.

The Jews, then, were expelled in 1290, but the powerful church and state did not only persecute those of a different religion. In the later 14th and 15th centuries, more than a hundred years prior to the Reformation, John Wycliffe (*c*.1324–84) and his followers, the Wycliffites or Lollards, caused immense concern to the established church. Wycliffe, an Oxford theologian, held many views at odds with then-contemporary church practice; he argued that priests (like Chaucer's Parson in *The Canterbury Tales*) should live simple lives and own no property.

The corruption of the church was at the forefront of social concerns at that time; the Peasants' Revolt in 1381 argued for some of the reforms Wycliffe had in mind. He maintained that there was no need for the church to control and mediate people's spiritual lives in the ways it did and that a lay priesthood should be permitted. He particularly advocated access to the Bible in the vernaculars of the people. Wycliffe found support among the nobility, including John of Gaunt—a patron of Chaucer's—some writers, and many ordinary Christians, who, after 1382, became known as Lollards. They began to be actively persecuted by anxious church authorities in the early 1400s. Wycliffite writings survive in Latin and in English, and include texts like *Pierce the Ploughman's Crede*, translations of the Bible, and many sets of sermons. Other writings, like the dialogue *Dives et pauper*, Langland's *Piers Plowman*, and, indeed, Chaucer's *Canterbury Tales*, have come under scholarly scrutiny in trying to detect Lollard sympathies.

# Chapter 8
# Consolidating literary traditions

## Singing of princes

Professional poets depended for their livelihood on their patrons and their skill. In all medieval literary contexts thus far, we have seen those who worked for the local nobility, or sometimes the king: the Anglo-Saxon *scop*, the Old Norse skald, the Welsh *Gogynfeirdd* (early poets), the Irish *file*, and the later Scottish *makar*. For the Celts, their poetic tradition was bardic; their practitioners, then as now, were *bards*. Across these earlier cultures, the teller of tales was important to the way society functioned and celebrated itself. The Anglo-Saxon poem *Deor*, written down in about 970, is a self-advertisement for its own poet and tells us a little about the status of the self-employed professional literary figure. The speaker, Deor, reveals that he was well employed until recently, with a loyal lord and rewards for his skill when he would sing with the harp, praising his patron. Now his job and his land have been given to a 'leoðcræftig monn' (man skilled in poetic craft), called Heorrenda: poetry was a competitive business.

In *Beowulf*, the Anglo-Saxon professional poet plies his trade in the king's hall where all the warriors gather for the feast, together with some of the noblewomen. The poet regales the assembled crowd with legends of heroes, like Sigemund the dragonslayer, and great wars or national events; he has a stock of learning and poetic formula at his disposal and he works deftly to create an engaging and pertinent verse narrative from his store of knowledge. Much of what the *scop* sings brings history into the present, and in so doing, creates a larger heroic context for Beowulf's exploits, or those of other warriors and kings.

Praise-poetry existed in all cultures, sung at the courts of kings and nobles to entertain, encourage, and gain renown and reward for the poet. The Old Norse skalds (see Box 9) of the Danish King Cnut's court in England (1016–35) wrote remarkable praise-poetry in honour of Cnut as the defeater of the English line of kings. Although this poetry was not written down until much later, there is no doubt of its creation being contemporary with Cnut himself. One of these skalds, Óttarr svarti, writes about the dynastic takeover that Cnut effected in 1016 when he took over the kingdom from Edmund Ironside, grandson of Edgar the Peaceable:

| | |
|---|---|
| Herskjöld bart ok helduð | You carried the warshield |
| hilmir, ríkr af slíku; | prince, and prevailed; |
| hykkat, þengill, þekkðust | I do not think, lord, you |
| þik kyrrsetu mikla. | cared much for sitting in peace. |
| AEtt drap, Jóta dróttinn, | Lord of the Jótar [Cnut], struck the kin |
| Játgeirs í för þeiri; | of Edgar on that expedition; |
| þveit rakt—þrár est heitinn— | ruler's son [Cnut], you dealt them |
| þeim, stillis konr, illan. | a harsh blow; you are called defiant. |

In complex poetry, alliterating, condensed, and rhetorically powerful, Cnut's reputation as the greatest of warriors is consolidated through the piling up of kingly heroic references.

Analogous to skaldic poets in service to kings and their courts is the work of the early Welsh poets of perhaps the 6th century: Taliesin who wrote in praise of Urien, king of Rheged; and Aneirin, the author of *Y Gododdin*. These early exponents of poetic art influenced the metre and method of the creations of later poets, the 12th-century *beirdd y twysogion* ('bards of the

## Box 9 Old Norse literature

Like all medieval vernacular literary traditions, Old Norse literature existed in oral form well before it was recorded in writing. It has a complicated history, made more complex by the geographical and cultural range of Old Norse, which includes not just Britain and Ireland, but also all the Scandinavian countries, including Iceland and Greenland. Within Anglo-Saxon England, the similarity of Old Norse and Old English languages means that the influence of Old Norse after the 9th century is difficult to detect. Certainly, English writings of the 10th century and later contain Old Norse loanwords and some stylistic similarities have been noted. Later texts still, such as the 12th-century verse sermon cycle the *Ormulum*, and the 14th-century romance *Sir Gawain and the Green Knight*, are quite indebted to Scandinavian influences.

The first Anglo-Scandinavian king of England, Cnut, who reigned from 1016 to 1035, encouraged the production of Old Norse verse by highly specialized poets called skalds. Similarly, the earls and bishops of the Scottish Isles, such as Orkney, patronized and composed courtly poetry in the 12th and 13th centuries, which was captured in writing by the later medieval authors of Icelandic sagas and poetry. Indeed, the centuries-old settlement in the British Isles of many Scandinavians had an immeasurably important impact on English; many everyday words like 'skin', 'they', 'sister', 'law', and 'husband' are Old Norse in origin.

princes'). Among these was Cynddelw Brydydd Mawr ('the great poet', 1155–1200), court poet of Prince Madog ap Maredudd; and Gwalchmai ap Meilyr (1130–80), who wrote in praise of the king of Gwynedd, Owain. Some of these poets wielded considerable power and became significant members of the household.

Those who wrote the most highly elevated poetry—like the skalds and the Irish *filidh*—might have close relationships with their

patrons. And the level of sophisticated poetry that they wrote
was demanding not just of the poet, but also of his audience.
The expectation was clearly that those listening were able to
understanding elusive references, dense metaphor, and clever
collocation. Clearly, for this work, the most proficient and
highest class of poets was patronized by great and, sometimes,
royal households who would provide reward and a public space
for the poets to perform their work.

The practice of royalty and nobles maintaining their own poet
continued in Wales, Ireland, England, and Scotland throughout
the Middle Ages and into the early modern period. In Wales, after
the Conquest of 1282 and the death of the last prince, Llewelyn
ap Gruffydd, the patronage of poetry moved to the houses of the
gentry, who (together with members of the clergy) employed
the *cywyddwyr* (later medieval poets, who flourished from about
1300 into the 16th century) to compose for them. Great Welsh
poets in the later Middle Ages include not only Dafydd ap
Gwilym, but also Iolo Goch, Guto'r Glyn, Tudur Aled, and Lewys
Glyn Cothi. These poets wrote on a host of subjects, including
inspirational poems about the bravery of contemporary
Welshmen in battles. Iolo Goch's panegyric *Syr Hywel y Fwyall*
('Sir Hywel of the Axe') focuses on Sir Hywel ap Gruffudd's
defence of Criccieth Castle when 'he put a bridle on the French
king's head':

> Annwyl fydd gan ŵyl einiort,
> *He'll be loved by the gentle romancer,*
> aml ei feirdd, a mawl i'w fort.
> *his poets are many, his table is praised.*

This reference to Hywel as being a worthy subject for the
romancer (a writer of romance narrative), and a patron of many
poets, is a reminder, too, that just as the best writers had the most
generous patrons, so those patrons gathered together materials
from a variety of sources into books that they commissioned for

their household. There is no doubt that having the best poets writing for them and having the most accomplished literary figures among their households gave additional cultural and social status to the elite, and glorified their own learning and their achievements.

## 'Men take of it heed'

In the later 14th century, Geoffrey Chaucer was associated with the court of Richard II. As we saw, Chaucer wrote *The Book of the Duchess* for John of Gaunt; and the *Legend of Good Women* was written for Richard II's wife, Anne of Bohemia. Chaucer's contemporary, a fellow courtly writer and Privy Seal clerk, Thomas Hoccleve (1367–1426), produced his very popular work the *Regiment of Princes* in about 1410 for the future King Henry V. This poem instructs a prince, though a long series of examples, how to rule justly and legitimately. In directly addressing Henry V in the *Regiment*, Hoccleve reminds his royal patron:

> In al my book yee schul nat see ne fynde
> *Throughout my book you shall not see or find*
> That I youre deedes lakke or hem despreise.
> *That I lessen your deeds or fail to praise them.*

Hoccleve had other patrons, too, including Humphrey of Gloucester, youngest son of Henry IV, and some of these royal figures were patrons of numerous writers, especially writers whose works were written in English. There was a wide audience for vernacular writings, and English writers could thus assist in getting particular messages—intellectual or political—across.

Prior to his accession to the throne, Henry V commissioned the prolific poet and monk of Bury St Edmunds John Lydgate (*c.*1370–1451) to write *Troy Book*. This poem of over 30,000 lines, completed in eight years by 1420, tells a moralizing story of the Trojan wars, which builds on previous versions of the well-established theme. It also seeks to build a new narrative of rightful lineage for the Lancastrian line (Henry IV had usurped Richard II). Lydgate wrote hundreds of other texts, too, in a wide variety of genres and he, like Hoccleve, was fully aware of the debt owed to Chaucer in providing a firm setting for English as a major literary medium for public poetry. A portrait of Chaucer is included in one of the early manuscripts of Hoccleve's *Regiment of Princes*, which lends authority to Hoccleve's work.

Both Hoccleve and Lydgate praised Chaucer explicitly in their own works, demonstrating not only his recognized authority and brilliance, but also claiming validation as his successors. Indeed, Hoccleve claimed that Chaucer tried to teach him how to write poetry. Lydgate, on the other hand, never met Chaucer, but his own merits as a writer were quickly established. He followed his *Troy Book* with the *Siege of Thebes* in 1422 and both poems make a case for the worthiness of chivalry. His works included anti-Lollard writings, confirming his role as a major orthodox author in his own right, who helped to promote both the monarchy and the established church against opponents. To this end, his moral writings, his saints' lives, and his numerous other religious works, such as *The Life of Our Lady*, mark him out as one of the most productive authors of the late Middle Ages.

The impact of Chaucer's writing had a wide reach. Almost immediately his influence was felt in Scotland, with the composition of *The Kingis Quair* ('The King's Book'), apparently written by the Scottish King James I, after his capture at the age of 11 by the English in 1406. He was imprisoned for eighteen years, and writes about his experiences in this semi-autobiographical poem. *The Kingis Quair* shows that the writer knew Chaucer's oeuvre very well, and was familiar with Lydgate's *Temple of Glass*. The author writes a dedication to Chaucer and to John Gower, multilingual author of *Mirour de l'omme*, *Vox clamantis*, and *Confessio amantis*. James lauds their work and hopes to benefit from their association:

> Unto impnis of my maisteris dere,
> *To the poems of my dear masters,*
> Gowere and Chaucere, that on the steppis satt
> *Gower and Chaucer, so that on the steps sat*
> Of rethorike quhill thai were lyvand here,
> *Of rhetoric while they were living here*
> Superlative as poetis laureate
> *Superlative as poets laureate*
> In moralitee and eloquence ornate,
> *In morality and ornate eloquence,*
> I recommend my buk in lynis sevin,
> *I recommend my book in seven-line stanzas,*
> And eke thair saulis unto the blisse of Hevin.
> *And also their souls into the bliss of Heaven.*

He also commends their souls to heaven, while recommending his book to sit on the steps of the poets laureate. His use of seven-line stanzas—Rhyme Royal—emulated a form perfected by Chaucer in his romance *Troilus and Criseyde*. Like *The Knight's Tale* in Chaucer's *Canterbury Tales*, *The King is Quair* examines themes influenced by Boethius' *Consolation of Philosophy* and courtly love, but does so in a self-conscious and subjective mode of expression.

## The flowering of national literatures

The royal association with Scottish literature illustrated by the writing of *The Kingis Quair* led to an extensive commissioning or patronage of literary works within the Scottish court itself later in the 15th century. The courtly poets of Scotland were known as the *makars*, and they also make clear their debt to Chaucer, whom they sought to emulate in their own work. This group of scholar-poets included Robert Henryson (*c.*1460–1500), who produced a version of the *Orpheus and Euridice* myth, as well as fables, and, most notably, the *Testament of Cresseid*, which seeks to reconfigure Chaucer's *Troilus and Criseyde* by, among other aspects, completing the earlier work.

Henryson's contemporary William Dunbar (*c*.1460–1520), like his earlier English counterparts, was closely allied with the royal court; James IV of Scotland was patron of Dunbar, who became a public poet, writing religious and secular works, as well as satirical verse, addressed at a variety of targets. In his *Lament for the Makaris*, Dunbar eulogizes great poets that have preceded him, including Chaucer, Gower, Barbour, Robert Henryson, and others. In it, he laments the brevity of life and the pointlessness of worldly glory, recognizing—as so many other medieval texts do—that all humanity turns to dust; Death spares no one. Repeating the cohering refrain, every four lines, *Timor Mortis conturbat me* ('Fear of death disturbs me') he talks of Death as 'petuously devour | The noble Chaucer, of makaris flour, | The Monk of Bury, and Gower, all three' ('devouring noble Chaucer, the flower of poets, Lydgate and Gower, all three'), Dunbar simultaneously bemoans the passing of the great, while celebrating, in poetry, their eternal greatness. He writes himself into this long line of literary wonders in the production of this poem, which survives in a number of manuscript versions.

What is especially notable about Chaucer, Lydgate, and Hoccleve in this period from *c*.1390 is that they attest to a renewed vigour in English literary composition and transmission, but this is now a literary endeavour that is supported *in English* by kings and the aristocracy. These authors all built on the prose and poetry of earlier writers to adapt and transform well-loved narratives into contemporary works, many with political resonances, and many directly addressed to monarchs and nobles. As interesting is the popularity of these great stories more broadly. Whereas other works exist in only one copy (like the romance *Sir Gawain and the Green Knight* and the three religious texts in the same manuscript, *Cleanness*, *Pearl*, and *Patience*; or the 15th-century poem *Athelston*), the works of Chaucer, Lydgate, and Hoccleve and Langland's religious masterpiece *Piers Plowman* tend to survive in multiple copies, suggesting that numerous noble households, or ecclesiastical institutions, wanted to commission copies. The status of the book as a marker of culture and education led to significant demand, a demand that resulted from increased male and female literacy and that could be met in abundance once printing got underway from 1485 in Britain.

## Ordering books, writing lives

The role of women is critical in any discussion of the flowering of the arts and their commissioning of books is important throughout the centuries. In the earlier Middle Ages, King Alfred reveals that it was his *mother* who encouraged his love of the written word and sought to make literacy a desirable skill in her son while he was still a young prince. Queen Emma, wife of King Cnut, commissioned the writing of the *Encomium Emmae reginae* in the 1040s, some years after Cnut died, in order to promote herself and her husband's reputation (see Figure 7). This Latin praise-text in honour of the queen does all it can to depict Cnut and Emma in a glorious light, using classical sources to elevate its subjects and seeking, through its rhetoric, to protect the interests of the queen at a time when her power at court was coming to an end. The fact that this *Encomium* was written in Latin prose replete with Virgilian echoes suggests that Emma was herself learned, multilingual, and politically astute. From the known commissioning of texts, it is possible to deduce a considerable amount about the abilities of the intended audience, or, at least, the image those commissioners wish to project.

Religious materials were also written at the request of women. Ailred of Rievaulx wrote the Latin *De institutione inclusarum* in about 1160 for his sister and other religious women who separated themselves from the world in religious contemplation. Before about

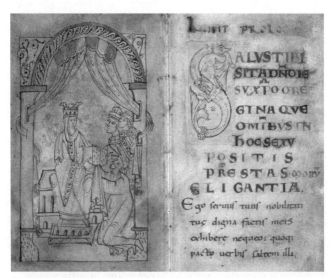

7. **London, British Library, Additional 33241, folio 1 verso.** *Encomium Emma Reginae* frontispiece.

1272, Friar Thomas Hales wrote his *Love-Ron* (*Love-Song*) after a religious woman, perhaps a nun, asked for a devotional song to encourage her in her chosen life as a virgin. Hales advises his addressee to sing the song about the rectitude of purity and the life of devotion to Christ in order to memorize it, to help her come to heaven where she would be led into the bridal chamber of God.

Throughout Britain and Ireland in the Middle Ages, increasing numbers of those families with money and some education made or commissioned whole books—anthologies of religious and secular verse and prose, often produced multilingually. One such book is the largest medieval literary book, the Vernon Manuscript now at the Bodleian Library in Oxford, compiled in around 1400 and containing 370 texts. It was written for someone, perhaps in the West Midlands, whose identity is not known, because their coat of arms in the manuscript was never completed.

Other owners are known, giving invaluable information about particular readers' interests. In Scotland, the Earl of Orkney commissioned the making of Oxford, Bodleian Library, Arch. Selden B. 24 in the 1480s, a manuscript of poetry that contains *The Kingis Quair*, alongside Hoccleve's *Mother of God*, and a good many Chaucerian poems including *Troilus and Criseyde*. This type of 'household' book was regularly produced from the closing years of the 14th century onwards, as it became more common for wealthy families to own manuscripts and documents, and, in many cases, participate in their creation.

The Findern Manuscript (Cambridge University Library, Ff. 1. 6), belonging originally to the Findern family in Derbyshire, and dated to the mid-15th century, shows the interests of women readers, whose names are written into the margins of the manuscript. The manuscript contains works by Chaucer and Gower, but also includes some lyrical poems that might have been written by women poets, one of which is a lament for the absence of a loved one.

Such absence is treated pragmatically by one of the writers in the Paston family, whose extensive collection of letters and legal documents gives a wonderful insight into life in the turbulent 15th century. These papers belonging to three generations of the family from Norfolk attests to the expansion and importance of literacy at this time. Among the family members was Agnes Paston, who in the 1440s and 1450s devoted time to writing to her children once they had left home. In her letters to her son John, who was living in London, she tells him all her gossip, recounting words she exchanged with angry neighbours and letting him know the local news. In lively (and my modernized) prose, she narrates that

> On Tuesday, Sir Jon Henyngham went to his church and heard
> three masses, and came home again never merrier, and said to
> his wife that he would go say a little devotion in his garden and then
> he would dine. And forthwith he felt a fainting in his leg and sat
> down. This was at nine of the clock, and he was dead before noon.

Other letters are less dramatic: Agnes informs John of the various legal cases with which she is involved; reminds him to settle his accounts; and sends him love and blessings. But these kinds of text, rare practical and everyday demonstrations of literacy, remind us of the lives and concerns of real medieval people, whose lives we can indirectly detect in the vibrant and diverse poetry and prose that forms the great canons of British and Irish literature.

# Chapter 9
# Coda: print and the canon

When William Caxton brought printing to London in 1485 from the continent where it had been flourishing for some thirty years, his choice to print in the vernaculars of England—English and French—consolidated the linguistic decisions made by many manuscript authors and compilers for hundreds of years. It was a choice based on the knowledge that this new textual tradition would thrive among the middle-class and aristocratic populace whose literacy was more assured in their own languages than in the scholarly Latin of centuries past.

As significant as language choice, though, were Caxton's actual selections of the texts to be printed in English in England. In choosing to publish Chaucer's *Canterbury Tales* and Malory's *Le Morte Darthur*, Caxton helped to consolidate what would go on to become fundamental works in the English literary canon. Since Malory's manuscript of *Le Morte Darthur* was lost after being used by Caxton until its extraordinary rediscovery at Winchester College in 1934 (see Figure 8), Caxton's printed edition also meant that the romance remained in circulation for the intervening centuries. In his Preface to the edition of *Le Morte Darthur*, Caxton reveals that he

> had accomplished and finished divers histories as well of contemplation as of other historial and worldly acts of great conquerors and princes, and also certain books of ensamples and doctrine.

Fter that I had accomplysshed and fynysshed dyuers
hystoryes as wel of contemplacyon as of other hysto
ryal and worldly actes of grete conquerours ⁊ pryn
ces / And also certeyn bookes of ensaumples and doctryne /
Many noble and dyuers gentylmen of thys royame of Eng
lond camen and demaunded me many and ofttymes / wherfore
that I haue not do made ⁊ enprynte the noble hystorye of the
saynt greal / and of the moost renomed crysten kyng / Fyrst
and chyef of the thre best crysten and worthy / kyng Arthur /
whyche ought moost to be remembrid emonge vs englysshe
men tofore al other crysten kynges / For it is notoyrly knowen
thorugh the vnyuersal world / that there ben ix worthy ⁊ the
best that euer were / That is to wete thre paynyms / thre Iewes
and thre crysten men / As for the paynyms they were tofore the
Incarnacyon of Cryst / whiche were named / the fyrst Hector
of Troye / of whome thystorye is comen bothe in balade and in
prose / The second Alysaunder the grete / ⁊ the thyrd Iulyus
Cezar Emperour of Rome of whome thystoryes ben wel kno
and bad / And as for the thre Iewes whyche also were tofore
thyncarnacyon of our lord of whome the fyrst was Duc Io
sue whyche brought the chyldren of Israhel in to the lond of
byheste / The second Dauyd kyng of Ierusalem / ⁊ the thyrd
Iudas Machabeus of these thre the byble reherceth al theyr no
ble hystoryes ⁊ actes / And sythe the sayd Incarnacyon haue
ben thre noble crysten men stalled and admytted thorugh the
vnyuersal world in to the nombre of the ix beste ⁊ worthy / of
whome was fyrst the noble Arthur / whos noble actes I pur
pose to wryte in thys present book here folowyng / The second
was Charlemayn or Charles the grete / of whome thystorye is
had in many places bothe in frensshe and englysshe / and the
thyrd and last was Godefray of boloyn / of whos actes ⁊ lyf
I made a book vnto thexcellent prynce and kyng of noble me
morye kyng Edward the fourth / the sayd noble Ientylmen
Instantly requyred me temprynte thystorye of the sayd noble
kyng and conquerour kyng Arthur / and of his knyghtes
wyth thystorye of the saynt greal / and of the deth and endyng
of the sayd Arthur / Affermyng that I ought rather tenprynte
his actes and noble featis / than of godefroye of boloyne / or

ij

8. William Caxton's *Preface* to his printed edition of Thomas Malory's *Le Morte Darthur*.

He recounts the other great heroes—the Nine Worthies (Hector, Alexander the Great, Julius Caesar; Joshua, David, and Judas Maccabeus; Charlemagne, Godfrey of Bouillon, and Arthur), who populate the great tales of the period. But denying the accusations of fiction made against Arthur and his legends, however, Caxton recognizes Arthur as 'first and chief of the Christian men'. He privileges the 'Matter of Britain', and the truth of a good story.

Like Chaucer in his *Retraction*, Caxton claims that 'all is written for our doctrine'; that is, he publishes the works he prints for the education of the audience, who should 'do after the good and leave the evil'. In choosing the good, he helped establish the excellence of early literary culture as it moved from manuscript to print and from the Middle Ages to a renaissance. The medieval in all of its manifestations has never subsequently ceased to fascinate, instruct, delight, shock, engage, move, and inspire.

# Further reading

## Introduction: endings and beginnings

Carruthers, G., and L. McIlvanney (ed.), *The Cambridge Companion to Scottish Literature* (Cambridge: Cambridge University Press, 2012).

Crawford, Robert, *Scotland's Books: The Penguin History of Scottish Literature* (London: Penguin, 2012).

Gantz, Jeffrey, *Early Irish Myths and Sagas* (London: Penguin, 1982).

Lapidge, Michael, *Anglo-Latin Literature, 900–1066* (London: Hambledon Press, 1972).

Pearsall, D., *Old and Middle English Poetry*, The Routledge History of English Literature I (London: Routledge, 1977).

Rigg, A. G., *A History of Anglo-Latin Literature, 1066–1422* (Cambridge: Cambridge University Press, 2006).

Williams, Gwyn (ed. and trans.), *The Burning Tree: Poems from the First Thousand Years of Welsh Verse* (London: Faber and Faber, 1956).

## Chapter 1: Literary origins

Pulsiano, Phillip and Elaine Treharne (eds.), *A Companion to Anglo-Saxon Literature* (Oxford: Wiley-Blackwell, 2001).

Solopova, Elizabeth and Stuart D. Lee, *Key Concepts in Medieval Literature*, Palgrave Key Concepts (London: Palgrave Macmillan, 2007).

Treharne, Elaine (ed.), *Anthology of Old and Middle English, c.890–1450*, 3rd edn (Oxford: Wiley-Blackwell, 2009).

Wallace, David (ed.), *The Cambridge History of Medieval English Literature* (Cambridge: Cambridge University Press, 1999).

## Chapter 2: Textual production and performance

Galloway, Andrew (ed.), *The Cambridge Companion to Medieval English Culture* (Cambridge: Cambridge University Press, 2011).

Hanna III, Ralph, *Introducing English Medieval Book History*, Exeter Medieval Texts and Studies (Exeter: Exeter University Press, 2013).

Johnson, David and Elaine Treharne (eds.), *Readings in Medieval Texts: Interpreting Old and Middle English Literature* (Oxford: Oxford University Press, 2005).

Owen-Crocker, Gale (ed.), *Working with Anglo-Saxon Manuscripts* (Exeter: Exeter University Press, 2009).

Treharne, Elaine and Greg Walker (eds.), *The Oxford Handbook to Medieval Literature in English* (Oxford: Oxford University Press, 2010).

## Chapter 3: Literary spaces, literary identities

Clanchy, M., *From Memory to Written Record*, 3rd edn (Oxford: Wiley-Blackwell, 2013).

Johnston, Dafydd, and Richard Loomis (trans.), *Medieval Welsh Poems: An Anthology* (Binghamton, NY: Medieval and Renaissance Texts and Studies, 1992).

Lees, Clare (ed.), *The Cambridge History of Early Medieval English Literature* (Cambridge: Cambridge University Press, 2013).

Manguel, Alberto, *A History of Reading* (London: Penguin, 1996).

Ní Bhrolcháin, Muireann, *Introduction to Early Irish Literature* (Dublin: Four Courts Press, 2009).

Taylor, Andrew, *Textual Situations: Three Medieval Manuscripts and Their Readers* (Philadelphia: University of Pennsylvania Press, 2002).

## Chapter 4: Individual and community

Ashe, Laura, *Early Fiction in England* (London: Penguin, 2015).

Barron, W. R. J., *English Medieval Romance* (London: Longman, 1987).

Brown, Peter (ed.), *A Companion to Medieval English Literature and Culture, c.1350–c.1500* (Oxford: Wiley-Blackwell, 2009).

Fulton, Helen (ed.), *A Companion to Arthurian Literature* (Oxford: Wiley-Blackwell, 2009).

Hays, R., et al. (ed.), *Records of Early English Drama; Dorset &*
*Cornwall* (Toronto: Toronto University Press, 1999).

Johnston, Dafydd, *A Pocket Guide: The Literature of Wales* (Cardiff:
University of Wales Press, 1994).

Walker, Greg (ed.), *Medieval Drama: An Anthology* (Oxford:
Wiley-Blackwell, 2000).

Woolf, R., *The English Mystery Plays* (London: Routledge & Kegan
Paul, 1972).

## Chapter 5: The mighty and the monstrous

Burrow, J. A., *Essays on Medieval Literature* (Oxford: Clarendon
Press, 1984).

Cohen, Jeffrey Jerome, *Monster Theory: Reading Culture*
(Minneapolis: University of Minnesota Press, 1996).

Echard, Siân (ed.), *A Companion to Gower* (Cambridge: D. S. Brewer,
2004).

Fulk, R. D. (ed. and trans.), *The Beowulf Manuscript*, Dumbarton
Oaks Medieval Library (Cambridge, Mass.: Harvard University
Press, 2010).

Hibbard, Laura A., *Medieval Romance in England* (New York: Burt
Franklin, 1963).

Krueger, Roberta L. (ed.), *The Cambridge Companion to*
*Medieval Romance* (Cambridge: Cambridge University Press,
2000).

Sims-Williams, Patrick, *Irish Influence on Medieval Welsh Literature*
(Oxford: Oxford University Press, 2011).

Treharne, Elaine, *Gluttons for Punishment: The Drunk and Disorderly*
*in Old English Sermons*, The Annual Brixworth Lecture (Leicester:
University of Leicester, 2007).

## Chapter 6: Love and longing

Ashe, Laura, *Fiction and History in England, 1066–1200* (Cambridge:
Cambridge University Press, 2007).

Crane, Susan, *Insular Romance: Politics, Faith, and Culture in*
*Anglo-Norman and Middle English Literature* (Berkeley:
University of California Press, 1986).

Duncan, T. G. (ed.), *A Companion to the Middle English Lyric*
(Cambridge: D. S. Brewer, 2005).

Fein, Susanna (ed.), *Studies in the Harley Manuscript: The Scribes, Contents, and Social Contexts of British Library MS Harley 2253* (Kalamazoo, Mich.: Western Michigan University, 2000).

Field, P. J. C. (ed.), *Malory Le Morte Darthur*, 2 vols (Cambridge: D. S. Brewer, 2013).

Huws, Daniel, *Medieval Welsh Manuscripts* (Cardiff: University of Wales Press and National Library of Wales, 2000).

Kennedy, Ruth and Simon Meecham-Jones (eds.), *Writers of the Reign of Henry II: Twelve Essays*, The New Middle Ages (London: Palgrave Macmillan, 2006).

Klinck, Anne (ed.), *The Old English Elegies: A Critical Edition and Genre Study* (Montreal: McGill University Press, 2001).

Woolf, R., *English Religious Lyric in the Middle Ages* (Oxford: Clarendon Press, 1968; repr. 1998).

## Chapter 7: Death and judgement

Atkinson, Robert (ed. and tr.). *The Passions and the Homilies from Leabhar Breac: Text, Translation, and Glossary.* Todd Lecture Series II (Dublin: Royal Irish Academy, 1887).

Benson, Larry D. (ed.), *The Riverside Chaucer*, 3rd edn (Oxford: Oxford University Press, 1988).

Brooke, Rosalind and Christopher, *Popular Religion in the Middle Ages: Western Europe, 1000–1300* (London: Thames and Hudson, 1984).

Minnis, A. J., *Medieval Theory of Authorship: Scholastic Literary Attitudes in the Later Middle Ages* (London: Scolar Press, 1984).

Owst, G. R., *Preaching in Medieval England* (Cambridge: Cambridge University Press, 1926).

Spencer, Helen Leith, *English Preaching in the Late Middle Ages* (Oxford: Clarendon Press, 1993).

Wright, C. D., *The Irish Tradition in Old English Literature* (Cambridge: Cambridge University Press, 1993).

## Chapter 8: Consolidating literary traditions

Clancy, Thomas O. (ed.), *The Triumph Tree: Scotland's Earliest Poetry, 550–1350* (Edinburgh: Cannongate, 2008).

Edwards, A. S. G., *A Companion to Middle English Prose* (Cambridge: D. S. Brewer, 2004).

McCash, June Hall (ed.), *The Cultural Patronage of Medieval Women* (Athens, Ga.: University of Georgia Press, 1996).

Meale, Carole, *Women and Literature in Britain, 1150–1500* (Cambridge: Cambridge University Press, 1993).

Parry, Thomas, ed. *The Oxford Book of Welsh Verse* (Oxford: Oxford University Press, 1962).

Townend, Matthew (ed.), *Editions of Skaldic Poems: Skaldic Poetry of the Scandinavian Middle Ages*, 1 and 2 (Turnhout: Brepols, 2012).

Walker, David, *Medieval Wales* (Cambridge: Cambridge University Press, 1990; repr. 1999).

## Chapter 9: Coda: print and the canon

Hellinga, Lotte and J. B. Trapp (eds.), *The Cambridge History of the Book in Britain, Volume III: 1400–1557* (Cambridge: Cambridge University Press, 2000).

Kuskin, William, *Symbolic Caxton: Literary Culture and Print Capitalism* (Notre Dame, Ind.: University of Notre Dame Press, 2008).

Further reading

# Index

# SOCIAL MEDIA
# Very Short Introduction

# Join our community
www.oup.com/vsi

- Join us online at the official Very Short Introductions **Facebook** page.
- Access the thoughts and musings of our authors with our online **blog**.
- Sign up for our monthly **e-newsletter** to receive information on all new titles publishing that month.
- Browse the full range of Very Short Introductions online.
- Read **extracts** from the Introductions for free.
- Visit our library of **Reading Guides**. These guides, written by our expert authors will help you to question again, why you think what you think.
- If you are a teacher or lecturer you can order inspection copies quickly and simply via our website.